# Issues in Faculty Personnel Policies

Jon W. Fuller, *Editor*

## NEW DIRECTIONS FOR HIGHER EDUCATION

MARTIN KRAMER, *Editor-in-Chief*

Number 41, March 1983

Paperback sourcebooks in
The Jossey-Bass Higher Education Series

Jossey-Bass Inc., Publishers
San Francisco • Washington • London

Jon W. Fuller (Ed.).
*Issues in Faculty Personnel Policies*
New Directions for Higher Education, no. 41.
Volume XI, number 1.
San Francisco: Jossey-Bass, 1983.

**New Directions for Higher Education Series**
Martin Kramer, *Editor-in-Chief*

Copyright © 1983 by Jossey-Bass Inc., Publishers
and
Jossey-Bass Limited

Copyright under International, Pan American, and Universal
Copyright Conventions. All rights reserved. No part of
this issue may be reproduced in any form — except for brief
quotation (not to exceed 500 words) in a review or professional
work — without permission in writing from the publishers.

**New Directions for Higher Education** (publication number USPS
990-880) is published quarterly by Jossey-Bass Inc., Publishers.
*New Directions* is numbered sequentially — please order extra
copies by sequential number. The volume and issue numbers
above are included for the convenience of libraries. Second-class
postage rates paid at San Francisco, California, and at
additional mailing offices.

*Correspondence:*
Subscriptions, single-issue orders, change of address notices,
undelivered copies, and other correspondence should be sent to
*New Directions* Subscriptions, Jossey-Bass Inc., Publishers,
433 California Street, San Francisco, California 94104.

Editorial correspondence should be sent to the Consulting Editor,
Martin Kramer, 2807 Shasta Road, Berkeley, California 94708.

Library of Congress Catalogue Card Number LC 82-84187

International Standard Serial Number ISSN 0271-0560

International Standard Book Number ISBN 87589-949-8

Cover art by Willi Baum

Manufactured in the United States of America

# Ordering Information

The paperback sourcebooks listed below are published quarterly and can be ordered either by subscription or as single copies.

Subscriptions cost $35.00 per year for institutions, agencies, and libraries. Individuals can subscribe at the special rate of $21.00 per year *if payment is by personal check.* (Note that the full rate of $35.00 applies if payment is by institutional check, even if the subscription is designated for an individual.) Standing orders are accepted.

Single copies are available at $7.95 when payment accompanies order, and *all single-copy orders under $25.00 must include payment.* (California, Washington, D.C., New Jersey, and New York residents please include appropriate sales tax.) For billed orders, cost per copy is $7.95 plus postage and handling. (Prices subject to change without notice.)

To ensure correct and prompt delivery, all orders must give either the *name of an individual* or an *official purchase order number.* Please submit your order as follows:

*Subscriptions:* specify series and subscription year.
*Single Copies:* specify sourcebook code and issue number (such as, HE8).

Mail orders for United States and Possessions, Latin America, Canada, Japan, Australia, and New Zealand to:
    Jossey-Bass Inc., Publishers
    433 California Street
    San Francisco, California 94104

Mail orders for all other parts of the world to:
    Jossey-Bass Limited
    28 Banner Street
    London EC1Y 8QE

## New Directions for Higher Education Series
## Martin Kramer, *Editor-in-Chief*

HE1   *Facilitating Faculty Development,* Mervin Freedman
HE2   *Strategies for Budgeting,* George Kaludis
HE3   *Services for Students,* Joseph Katz
HE4   *Evaluating Learning and Teaching,* C. Robert Pace
HE5   *Encountering the Unionized University,* Jack H. Schuster
HE6   *Implementing Field Experience Education,* John Duley
HE7   *Avoiding Conflict in Faculty Personnel Practices,* Richard Peairs
HE8   *Improving Statewide Planning,* James L. Wattenbarger, Louis W. Bender
HE9   *Planning the Future of the Undergraduate College,* Donald G. Trites
HE10  *Individualizing Education by Learning Contracts,* Neal R. Berte
HE11  *Meeting Women's New Educational Needs,* Clare Rose
HE12  *Strategies for Significant Survival,* Clifford T. Stewart, Thomas R. Harvey
HE13  *Promoting Consumer Protection for Students,* Joan S. Stark

# Contents

# Editor's Notes

Most faculty personnel policies have developed over the years in response to specific needs, both institutional and individual. Revisions are usually made piecemeal, as specific problems or requirements arise. Faculty personnel issues are therefore too often treated as narrow and technical questions, and not as the important tool that they can be for an institution as it tries to meet its larger educational objectives.

Faculty personnel policies represent an intersection of institutional objectives and the needs of individual faculty members, and most existing policies represent the result of years of explicit or sometimes subtle negotiation.

Appropriate institutional objectives in setting faculty personnel policies are to recruit and retain appropriate and qualified faculty, to encourage continued professional growth and development, and to promote institutional loyalty and morale. In some of its policies, an institution may also wish to encourage some regular turnover to provide balance in the faculty and allow adaptation to shifting curricular needs. Institutions also want policies that will appropriately reflect institutional values. Individuals need to be treated in a fair and considerate way. No institution wants dissension and disruption because of personnel decisions. Increasingly important is the related need for institutions to maintain policies that will discourage legal challenges and provide a strong defense against those that do come.

Individual faculty members, as they look at institutional personnel policies, look for a place that will allow them to do worthwhile work. Most faculty members see their career as far more than just another job. Faculty and all employees want to be treated fairly and predictably, and to have their contributions and achievements recognized and rewarded. They also want stability and security for themselves and their families.

The themes of the next decade of higher education—declining enrollments, reduced resources, and changing student clienteles—are already discouragingly familiar. They present obvious new problems for colleges and universities, as well as some less obvious new opportunities. As institutions respond to new conditions, faculty personnel policies should be looked at anew, and changes made to adapt them to serve new institutional needs, as well as to sustain old and still-valued purposes.

1

To begin at the beginning, institutions need to recruit the best new faculty members — a task which Louis Brakeman reminds us in the first chapter is more difficult than some might expect. He suggests a number of specific and practical steps that can be taken, particularly in trying to attract female and minority candidates.

The pragmatic tone of the first chapter sets the tone for this volume. This is not primarily a research effort. Most of the authors are administrators, charged at their own institutions with carrying out the policies about which they write in this volume.

The specific and increasingly complex issues of faculty compensation are reviewed by Fred Silander, who brings to these issues the particularly appropriate credentials of an economist, a financial vice-president, and a former dean of faculty.

David Marker discusses leave policies in Chapter Three. This chapter illustrates the contradictory pressures on policies that result from changing conditions. On the one hand, financial restraints naturally suggest caution and some tightening up of requirements for leaves. At the same time, institutions need to be more concerned to renew and sustain the enthusiasm and competence of existing faculty. This requires a balancing act — which will more and more be the required posture for administrators as they set policies for the years ahead.

Evaluation of faculty is not new, as Kala Stroup reminds us. But the pressures for evaluation to be formal and explicit have increased. So have the stakes, both for the individual and the institution. But no system of evaluation seems quite satisfactory, probably because of the demands that evaluation serve several functions which are often at cross-purposes. In evaluation, to an unusual degree, who makes policies and how they are carried out can be as important in determining their effect as what they are. Her practical review of the issues will be useful in any reassessment of an institution's evaluation policies and practices.

Roger Baldwin looks at personnel policies in a new way, asking about the effects of various policies on the recently recognized need to provide variety and continued stimulation and challenge in the careers of faculty. In times of greater faculty mobility and readily available external grant support, faculty vitality might have been left to care for itself. Policies were shaped in those years to retain the best faculty and keep them at their jobs as long as possible, knowing that many would be lured away by other opportunities. But as Baldwin reminds us, we now need to look anew at policies about leaves, tenure, rewards, and course assignments, all with an eye to encouraging the good faculty who now remain with us for most of their careers to continue to be lively and effective teachers and scholars.

Retirement issues appropriately bring the volume to its close. These are reviewed by Francis King, a researcher, but one with long experience in higher education's principal retirement agency, Teachers Insurance and Annuity Association (TIAA). At the same time that many institutions are beginning to look at their retirement plans, with an eye to greater personnel flexibility, particularly through early and phased retirement options, the world of pensions and retirements has become more complex. New laws and regulations both restrict institutional discretion in setting policies, and also add new options which need to be considered.

One of the knottiest issues of faculty personnel policy, tenure, does not have its own chapter in this volume. Although the subject of much debate and analysis in recent years, few institutions are willing to pay the high cost of abandoning tenure, and most efforts to modify it through quotas or term contracts produce less change than meets the eye. There are issues about tenure which need to be addressed, of course, and those are treated from different perspectives by Brakeman, Stroup, and Baldwin in their chapters.

The special constraints of making and administering personnel policies in a collective bargaining situation are also not specifically addressed in this volume. The process is necessarily different, but many of the needs and purposes are not, and administrators working within a collective bargaining system will find the issues raised in this volume worth considering and adding to their bargaining agenda.

Above all, this volume seeks to take a new and comprehensive look at faculty personnel policies, linking them to larger changes which are beginning to affect both institutions and individual faculty.

Jon W. Fuller
Editor

*Jon W. Fuller is president of the Great Lakes Colleges Association (GLCA), a consortium of twelve liberal arts colleges in Indiana, Michigan, and Ohio. Under his leadership, GLCA has developed major consortial programs in faculty development, and has helped the member colleges explore problems and possibilities in the careers of their faculty members.*

*An active, assertive, and positive approach will attract*
*the best faculty, even if tenure cannot be guaranteed.*

# Hiring and Keeping
# the Best Faculty

*Louis F. Brakeman*

The dominant concern of young people searching for positions in higher
education is to find a job. Tenuring in, reduced flexibility, few opportunities for new faculty, and poor morale among young faculty who
have jobs are the worries of chairpersons and academic deans, presidents, and boards of trustees. These concerns are valid enough.

Attracting high quality faculty to the positions that do exist is a
concern as well. So is keeping young faculty in good spirits, satisfied in
their work, and optimistic about their future. All too often, even where
positions are open, talented candidates cannot be found, especially minority and women candidates. In an era when opportunities are few, it
may seem incongruous to emphasize the problem of attracting quality
candidates.

How to attract and keep the best qualified candidates, especially
women and minorities, is the challenge addressed in this chapter.

## The Illusion of a Buyer's Market

Fewer than five viable candidates were identified for a short-
term position in chemistry available for a recent year at a quality liberal

J. W. Fuller (Ed.). *Issues in Faculty Personnel Policies.* New Directions for
Higher Education, no. 41. San Francisco: Jossey-Bass, March 1983.

arts college in the Midwest. The department was fully tenured and with more faculty than justified so there could be not even a glimmer of hope for a tenurable position. The recruiting situation was even bleaker in computer science, where no fully qualified candidates applied for a tenurable position. In political science, a search was suspended after the department concluded that the candidates were not up to expected standards. In other areas some excellent candidates were recruited, interviewed, and hired but the judgment in those instances was that once one passed beyond a thin, top layer of outstanding persons, the quality of the applicants plummeted quickly.

These are anecdotes, to be sure. Yet conversations among chief academic officers, departmental chairpersons, and senior faculty from a variety of institutions of higher learning suggest that these experiences are far from unique. Given the demographic forecasts, the erosion of salaries in the face of inflationary pressures, the new demands at most institutions to teach students not as well prepared as in earlier years, the quickening pace of life for teacher-scholars, the vanishing number of tenurable positions, the extension of the mandatory retirement age to seventy, and cutbacks in funding at national and state levels, it is surprising that any talented, ambitious, self-assured men and women would choose a career in higher education. Obviously, there is wide variation among disciplines. Even where the demand for graduates is great, as in engineering and computer science, for example, many of the best students are not considering teaching, or even getting the Ph.D., but rather are moving directly from the master's degree into industrial positions. In the humanities and social sciences, the demand for faculty is minimal and the undergraduate honors students who once might have gone on to emulate their mentors are now not even considering graduate school.

Hard data to document these impressions are not readily available, but many hiring officers are convinced they are accurate. In this chapter, we will describe briefly some of the particular problems in recruiting talented faculty and suggest some strategies and some specific steps in dealing with those problems. The focus of the analysis will be the independent, quality liberal arts colleges, although the problems and the solutions will be characteristic of many institutions of higher learning.

## Basic Strategies

This analysis makes two basic assumptions. One is that there are qualified people, at least a few really good candidates, who want an academic career. The other is that education is one of our most crucial tasks as a society and that the need for committed, fully qualified people will continue. In other words, it is worth making the effort to attract good candidates. Candidates are available. The need continues to be real. Even so, the task is not easy.

The essence of the approach to attracting excellent faculty is to take an active, assertive, positive approach. A passive, laid back, wait-and-see strategy is insufficient. Having a clear sense of the positive charactersitics of the position for which the recruitment is being under-taken is of central importance. Obviously certain types of colleges and departments will not appeal to everyone. The effort of the recruiter ought to be clear and convincing about the challenges, the excitement, the satisfactions, and even the joys to be found in a particular position. From the candidate's point of view, a place ought to appear attractive, worthwhile, and able to provide an opportunity to develop some com-petencies, to advance one's career, and to have a satisfying life. How the case is made, of course, will vary from college to college, depart-ment to department, and even from position to position.

The attractions of a particular position need to be identified and explained concisely and positively. If the position, department, or insti-tution is not attractive, the task will be difficult. If such is the case, then the effort to recruit excellent faculty must deal first with the need to im-prove the situation to which one hopes to attract new recruits.

Each institution and each department has a certain character, a tone, and an environment. Some are conservative, unfriendly, rigid, and uninviting. A place that is vital, open to new ideas, full of life, working to balance tradition and change, and responsive to new intel-lectual currents, with a president and chief academic officer who em-body these characteristics, will be more likely to be attractive to the best candidates than a place that is dormant, closed, conservative, and run in a heavy-handed fashion. To be blunt, in some instances there may well be an elemental need to start by placing key leaders at the top who have a positive, open attitude and who work interactively and sys-tematically to infuse an institution with the qualities that will attract fine candidates. A college with weaknesses in the key leadership posi-tions may not be able to attract the best candidates no matter what strategies are used.

Tenured positions are more likely to attract the best candidates, of course, but these may not be feasible in many colleges and depart-ments. Renewable, non-tenurable positions extending from two to six or seven years is the typical alternative, although a few places are try-ing contracts that extend beyond the conventional seven-year probationary period. Dealing with this issue requires comprehensive personnel planning on a departmental and collegewide basis. Certain aspects of this planning are addressed elsewhere in this book.

Early and phased retirement plans and career exploration opportunities may result in tenured positions opening up in departments that otherwise look very closed to change. Careful monitoring of enrollments both overall and by relevant units (departments, divisions, or whatever) will enable a chief academic officer to make an informed judgment about the tenurability of a particular position. Judicious estimates of possible resignations can also be useful. Some places are now indicating up front and in writing that while a position is tenurable, so-called environmental factors will be considered on the occasion of contract renewal. Enrollment patterns and departmental and college needs and plans are being accepted as appropriate considerations in decisions about renewal and tenure. A departmental chairperson and chief academic officer should talk frankly with candidates about the particular circumstances surrounding the position available. Many candidates appreciate such frankness and are realistic enough to know that rarely will a circumstance be ideal from their point of view. If the chances for tenure seem not totally negative, they may well be impressed by candor, by attention to the future, and by the goodwill and concern reflected in the effort to provide an assessment of the future.

In some instances there may be flexibility to permit a joint appointment to two departments or to a department and an interdepartmental program. In other cases, an administrative appointment to head a program or a curriculum-related office might provide a rationale for the prospect of a relationship longer than seven years.

One of the most powerful attractions will be the people with whom the candidate will work. Obviously, one cannot do much about the faculty already present. Assuming that they are a stimulating group of people, certain specific activities ought to occur as part of the recruitment process. One of the most engaging, articulate, and knowledgeable faculty ought to do interviewing at any convention-related recruiting site. On campus, the candidate ought to see most, if not all, departmental faculty individually. Also, in addition to a rigorous question-and-answer setting, there should be an informal social setting as well. The chief academic officer, or the appropriate collegewide official responsible for hiring, should be on the interview schedule as should faculty from other departments who have an interest in the candidate's teaching and/or research area.

In some colleges, campuswide, extradepartmental interviewing is done as a part of the regular interviewing process. If this is not done regularly, the involvement of selected faculty will provide insight about the nature of contacts the person will enjoy. Interviewing outside the department can be particularly useful in the recruitment of women or minority candidates, who will need to understand the special problems and opportunities they will face in a particular college setting. Faculty ought to talk about their own research and teaching interests and share the excitement they feel about their work. Students, of course, should be included as well, especially junior and senior majors, and perhaps even a committee should be selected for the specific purpose of interviewing candidates. The reader will know of, or can imagine, specific activities appropriate to her or his own campus, ones that will convey to candidates something of what it would be like to work there.

The Academy for Educational Development published a booklet in October 1982 (Tickton) which consists of brief descriptions of over 100 specific programs and activities designed to attract and retain faculty. Examples come from a wide range of institutions; some are very expensive, others are not.

## Two-Career Couples and Joint Appointments

Two-career couples are becoming more common in our society. Colleges in relatively isolated areas find it increasingly difficult to attract the best candidates when a spouse is also pursuing a career. There is no easy solution to the challenge posed by this circumstance; it is rarely within the competence of a particular college to offer two full-time jobs within the areas of ability of the couple. Circumstances vary considerably and so, therefore, do possible responses.

In the recruitment process it is not proper to inquire about the spouse, nor to suggest that considerations about the spouse or about residence are germane to a decision. Not only are such considerations inappropriate from the nondiscrimination point of view, but bringing up such topics is apt to repel candidates one would like to attract. One should be helpful but should not pry and should not be judgmental.

The spouse of the preferred candidate may have a career outside higher education. In this circumstance, a hiring officer could point out possibilities for employment and could facilitate the search by the spouse. If the college is located outside an urban area, the spouse may have to find a position some considerable distance from the college. Residence then becomes a problem and the college will need to come to terms with whether to insist on residence close to the college. One does so at the risk of losing candidates even though geographic proximity to the campus has important advantages in terms of faculty-student relationships and involvement in the community by the faculty member. Traditional attitudes toward residency may have to give way, however, if talented two-career couples are to be recruited successfully.

The residency issue may be germane even if the spouse is in higher education and finds a position at a nearby college. The difficulties are magnified if the distance between the jobs requires two residences and long, infrequent, or weekend-only commutes. Then there will need to be tolerance for the amount of time a person may be away from campus. Certainly many two-career couples will not expect, and may even resent, special treatment. They will expect to work hard, and to do as well as persons who do not face the two-career challenge. Even so, there is no doubt that the tensions and the difficulties of coping with everyday living are greater for a two-career family, especially if there are children. So, while it is important that equity exist, at least sensitivity to the particular challenges of two-career families will be appreciated. When this sensitivity is obvious to candidates, they may be more attracted to that campus. Efforts to support and to accommodate two-career families will attract persons who otherwise would go elsewhere. At a minimum, attitudes of understanding and concern and a willingness to help in ways that do not violate college or other policies ought to be adopted.

The complexities of such arrangements still cause most institutions to limit themselves to more conventional and familiar terms of appointment. But many institutions have been willing to make such appointments in order to attract the candidates they most want. As a result, there are now a number of examples of joint or shared appointments that have worked satisfactorily, and that can be drawn upon to work out an attractive offer. The participants in such an appointment may be husband and wife; they may be two unrelated individuals.

One model, in effect, considers the couple as one person. Under another model a husband and wife may each be considered a part-time faculty member and the conditions of employment for part-time faculty apply. In some colleges, tenure is possible for part-time faculty, usually with a longer probationary period than for full-time faculty. Benefits are treated in different ways. In some cases benefits are prorated; in others full benefits apply provided half-time or more employment exists. In some instances the couple fills one position in a particular department. The couple may together be full-time, but hold part-time positions in different academic departments or different offices. Some of the details will vary depending on whether the two people are married or not. Here are some of the considerations involved in a joint appointment.

*Responsibilities and Privileges*

The case of joint appointments requires special attention to the responsibilities and privileges of each person.

1. The actual division of courses and teaching time by term is negotiated according to the needs of the department and the preferences/competencies of the individuals.

2. Each person has the privileges and responsibilities of a full-time person. For example, each supervises individual student work, advises students, is eligible for membership on college and departmental committees, votes in departmental and faculty meetings, and is eligible for support for professional grants and attendance at workshops. (The time commitment expected of the two persons ought not exceed what is normally expected of one individual. This is potentially a problem area. Certainly the time commitment of faculty varies considerably. Exploitation must be avoided on the one hand, and, on the other hand, the impulses of each person need to be restrained. Making an arrangement of this sort requires an atmosphere of trust, openness, and candor. The individuals must restrain any tendency to work full-time and the chairperson must restrain herself or himself and even protect the couple from demands by others both within the department and from the wider community.)

3. Work elsewhere may be permitted provided the two assignments do not exceed a normal full-time load according to the standards of the primary college. Also it should be understood that the assignment will not preclude the person's fulfillment of normal additional professional responsibilities, such as advising and committee service.

*Termination, Reappointment, and Tenure*

1. Should one person resign, one way to deal with the situation is to declare the position open and permit the remaining person to compete for it with other candidates.

2. In considering the person for various forms of reappointment, the usual approach is to consider the persons as a team. Decisions should be made according to the conventional criteria.

3. If the team fails because of the unsuitability of one member of the team, one approach is to consider the position open. The other member of the team could then apply for the open position.

4. In the event an additional tenurable position in the department becomes available, departmental needs at that time should determine how that position should be filled. Participants in the joint appointment could be, but need not be, given priority in that consideration.

*Salary and Staff Benefits*

1. Each person is paid one-half the total salary.
2. Benefit arrangements need to be worked out in accordance with general policy. Benefits directly related to salary can be shared half and half. Medical insurance is available to both persons as is tuition assistance for children. Other benefits, such as sabbatical leaves and travel allowances, are handled on an individual basis with some reduction from full-time terms. Certain legislatively mandated benefits apply individually. In the case of two unrelated individuals, full medical coverage and contribution to retirement for both is normal. For other than mandated benefits, the benefit policy for part-time faculty probably would apply.

## Obligations To Faculty Who Cannot Be Retained

A hard-nosed, tough approach might well be expected from administrators toward faculty who cannot be retained. This conventional attitude still may be appropriate toward those terminated for cause or perhaps even for those hired for one or two years as leave replacements. The concern here, however, is particularly for those who would be retained were it not for concern about flexibility necessary to respond to demographic and enrollment and related concerns. Institutions do have a special obligation toward these people. Letting candidates know about the assumption of that obligation may assist in attracting faculty who would otherwise not accept an offer.

The specific forms of support that might be offered are fairly straightforward. However, the attitude or disposition of the chief administrators and of the faculty is most crucial. The conventional attitude of most administrators is to justify any assistance to a faculty member in terms of the eventual benefit to the college. The most common expression of this view is that we do not "owe" a sabbatical to a faculty member. Sabbaticals are justified in terms of how faculty members will improve their competence to serve back at the college. This traditional attitude, when extended to nontenured faculty (especially those who cannot be retained), would result in little sympathy for support for those who will not continue to teach at the college. New attitudes are appropriate and a demonstration by the administration to show it is committed to assisting faculty in the progress of their careers, even where there can be no direct institutional benefit, will make a college attractive to some candidates even if the prospect for tenure is not bright.

Chief academic officers can take several steps to assist a person who has done well but who cannot be retained. They can:

1. Write a letter commenting on the person's work.

2. Recommend the person to other chief academic officers.

3. Provide a lightened teaching load at a time when the person is searching for a new position.

4. Provide limited financial assistance: payment of travel and hotel costs, for example, of at least one professional meeting.

5. After full consultation with the person, provide those experiences the person thinks would be useful in expanding his or her competencies (a particular committee assignment, a temporary, part-time administrative appointment, or attendance at an appropriate workshop).

6. Assign fewer than the normal number of advisees.

7. Discourage the person from taking on time-consuming committee and/or special interest responsibilities. (Many young faculty seek out such activity and are good at it. However, many over-extend themselves partly because they think they are expected to take on such work.)

8. Provide a teaching schedule (types of courses) that will enhance the attractiveness of the person to other institutions. Responsibility for teaching only the introductory course, for example, should be avoided.

Imaginative chief academic officers will find additional ways to be of help. In some instances, given the right circumstances and with some advanced planning, it might be possible to offer an especially talented person a full-time administrative appointment if that would be seen as mutually desirable. It could well be useful to the young faculty person to have an open-ended conversation about careers. In some instances a young person who is questioning continuing in an academic career could be helped to explore his or her competencies, interests and preferences in a systematic way. Such an exploration might be in a consultation with a sympathetic, skilled career counselor or in a workshop. Whatever form it might take, financial support and released time for such activity would be useful and appropriate.

In summary, a chief academic officer can assist a young person in enhancing her or his career. An environment that will enhance the marketability of a young teacher-scholar who cannot be retained can be created. The existence of such an environment could well attract a talented candidate who welcomes a supportive community.

## Research Support for the Young Scholar

The existence of special research assistance could attract especially talented candidates and be particularly useful to junior faculty.

Some institutions have established special research programs available only to young faculty. Several of these are described in the *1982 Idea Handbook* referred to earlier. For example, the University of California at Berkeley supplies money and staff to young faculty members for field research in the natural and social sciences (Tickton, p. 28). On a more modest level, a small college might set aside funds from a locally funded professional development budget for nontenured faculty—or might give priority to these persons. One way of stretching limited resources is to give lower priority to those faculty who have received grants the previous years. Such support not only permits a young person to build up her or his credentials, but if the supported work is appropriately designed, it can provide personal contacts beyond the campus and develop a track record for applying for further grants from foundations or government sources.

A unique program for young scholars who have their contracts terminated while engaged in research projects has been established by the Five Colleges, Incorporated (Amherst, Hampshire, Mount Holyoke, Smith, and the University of Massachusetts). A brief description of this program is included in the *1982 Idea Handbook* (Tickton, p. 98). The research associates program offers two-year appointments for faculty whose contracts have been terminated or who are having difficulty finding employment. "These appointments offer: (a) an academic affiliation, (b) access to all five library systems, (c) office space, (d) medical insurance, (e) access to seminars and lectures, (f) the collegiality of faculty in their fields, and (g) temporary teaching assignments at their institutions."

An incentive program is also included in the program of Five Colleges, Incorporated, to encourage faculty to take early retirement. These people would also be associated with the program. While the benefits of this program arise from the close proximity and diversity of the five schools, it is conceivable that other clusters of institutions might undertake a similar effort.

Special research programs for younger faculty, including released time and summer support, exist at several colleges including Macalester, Oberlin, and Wabash. Special funds to support attendance at workshops and specialized conferences, to consult with research colleagues, and to take advantage of special opportunities also can be useful. Released time to complete a dissertation or an article for publication can be provided at fairly low cost and can be a great advantage to a young scholar attempting to establish a respectable initial record of scholarship or other creative effort.

## Recruiting Strategies for Women and Minorities

Particular issues arise in the effort to recruit and hire women and minorities. A demonstrated commitment to make special efforts to recruit and hire women and minorities and to provide a satisfying environment for them is an essential prerequisite to a successful effort. In certain fields, of course, there are ample numbers of women candidates; in others, there are not. There are *far* fewer minority candidates in most disciplines, as national availability figures suggest (Corbitt, 1978; "Fact File...," 1982).

Women and minorities are especially apt to want to know if the environment of a place will be supportive of their presence. Some may not much care, but a college that seeks to increase the proportion of women and minorities on the faculty is well advised to pay special attention to issues related to tone, ambience, and environment. Do clear signals abound that tell women and minorities that they are second class? If so, this will be perceived by talented candidates, and they will go elsewhere.

An affirmative action plan, even if not required, establishes a commitment to the establishment of an equitable environment. An active, respected affirmative action officer, even if part-time, furthers the commitment.

First and foremost, the tone must be set by the president and chief academic officer. They should make their expectations clear, and insist that goals be set, and ask for reports. Especially vigorous action should be taken when information suggests that a strong pool of women/minority candidates exists. These concerns and follow-up activities should be made known publicly enough so that candidates will learn about them. In certain instances, the president or chief academic officer may want to become personally involved in generating candidates by talking with prospective candidates, telling them about the college, and, if appropriate, encouraging them to apply.

The views of women and minorities on issues and concerns must be respected and considered valid. Manifestations of sexism and racism must be dealt with promptly. A grievance procedure must be in place and usable. A committee or support group organized by women and by minorities should be encouraged. Depending on the circumstances a special ad hoc, informal group may meet, headed by the president or other chief administrative officer to deal with ongoing racial concerns. The presence of a women's studies and ethnic or black studies program will help.

Florence Howe, one of the early leaders in women's studies and codirector of the Feminist Press, provides a good summary of the characteristics of a campus environment healthy for women (Howe, 1982, pp. xii–xvi). To be healthy for women, a campus must have women faculty and administrators, and needs to provide opportunities for women and students to take on leadership positions, to engage in intercollegiate sports if they choose, to take courses that address issues of particular concern to women, and so on. So to be truly effective in recruiting women faculty, a good deal of prior work may be necessary to develop an environment women faculty will find supportive and enriching. In fact, as numbers of women on the faculty and administrative staff increase, tensions may well mount as issues and concerns are brought into the open. A critical mass may be necessary before issues of sexism, overt or covert, are challenged. When this happens, strategies will need to be devised to meet the concerns and to advance the cause of a truly equitable environment.

### How to Recruit

Here are several specific ideas that have worked: Advertisements must appear in the appropriate professional outlets, and, for national searches, in *The Chronicle of Higher Education.* Advertising in *The Black Scholar* may be useful. (Some special publications, including disciplinary job lists, have prepublication deadlines of up to sixty days.) Women and black caucuses vary considerably in their effectiveness. Some maintain current lists of candidates and are well equipped to spread the word about openings; others are not. Advertisements may include the phrase "Women and minorities are encouraged to apply."

Networking is invaluable. As long as a position is widely and openly advertised there is no reason why networking cannot be actively used. In minority recruitment especially, one can contact previous visitors to campus, minority trustees or those close to a minority community, alumni, and friends of the college. Former students in graduate school or holding academic appointments may be especially helpful. The Urban League and the churches from which students come may know of persons who could be candidates. In generating women candidates, as well, acquaintances should be contacted, perhaps even by the appropriate academic dean.

Here are a few additional specific tips especially for attracting minority candidates.

1. Do not suppose that minority candidates will not want to teach in a predominantly white college or to live in a predominantly

white community. Some will find this difficult, of course. Others may in fact prefer the less hectic environment and the emphasis on teaching offered by small, quality liberal arts colleges located in small towns.

2. Learn to recognize the names of black colleges and universities and fraternities and sororities and to evaluate their quality. In fact, contacts with the national offices of black fraternities and sororities may be useful.

3. Offer black candidates who come to campus for an interview an opportunity to meet informally with other black professional staff and faculty (if any). Also offer to set up a gathering with black students, possibly through the black student organization. However, do not assume that the candidate wants to do this; some will prefer not to do so.

In some cases it may be fitting for an appropriate person to have a conversation on the telephone, in person, or at a convention with particularly attractive candidates. The very taking of such an initiative will convey a sense of commitment.

In advertisements, the position ought to be defined, to the extent feasible, in terms of competencies sought. Academic competencies/ fields ought to be defined so as not to exclude women, but rather to encourage them to apply. While not all women economists, for example, would be attracted by an advertisement that suggested that "Women in the Labor Force" could be a teaching field, some would.

There are a few organizations and programs that may be of assistance. There is a minority fellowship program at Indiana University. While primarily a fellowship program, it is also a clearinghouse for minorities with Ph.D.s seeking jobs and colleges recruiting minorities. There are social science, humanities, and science parts of the program, although it is relatively new and only students in the social sciences area are, as of 1982–83, at the completed Ph.D. level.

The National Association for Equal Opportunity has sponsored a national conference on blacks in higher education. While much of the focus of the 1982 conference was the promotion of historically black colleges and universities, there was also considerable discussion of the recruitment and retention of black faculty at predominantly white schools. The job fair at the conference excluded participation by white campuses, but even should this practice continue, the presence at such conferences of a person or persons from a white college, particularly if that person is black, does afford an opportunity to make known the existence of positions and to spread the word about the college.

Another approach to building a black presence on campus is through exchange of faculty, either with black institutions in the South or with African institutions. A visiting professorship is another possibility, or perhaps a joint appointment with a nearby university. Key people need to be alert to possible candidates, even if positions are not immediately available, and the appropriate departments and administrators need to be flexible enough to depart from normal staffing patterns when an outstanding opportunity is identified.

Several of the above steps would be useful, with modification, in attracting women candidates. Visiting women scholars could be brought to campus for brief stays, to consult with faculty and students and to serve later as a point of contact as positions become available. Women who come to interview should meet women faculty and administrators and be offered the opportunity to meet with women's studies faculty and members of the local women's support group. In the total interview process, be absolutely certain that statements and procedures that could be seen as sexist are avoided. The same advice applies to interviewing minority candidates.

Of central importance in recruiting women and minorities is a firm commitment by the president and chief academic officer which is backed by the board of trustees. This commitment must be expressed in specific actions that are clear to all concerned.

## Conclusion

In summary, while good candidates may be hard to find, they do exist. Thoughtful, innovative, well-organized efforts encouraged by presidents and chief academic officers will attract the best candidates, even if tenure cannot be guaranteed. Conventional attitudes and practices will need to yield to new ways of thinking and behaving. This chapter has suggested some examples of those new approaches.

## References

Corbitt, G. I. *Availability Data in Academic Professions and Related Occupations,* 2nd ed. Boulder, Colo.: The University of Colorado, 1978.
"Fact File, A Profile of 1980–81 Recipients of Doctorates." *Chronicle of Higher Education,* October 6, 1982, p. 8.
Howe, F. "Everywoman's Educational Health." In F. Howe, S. Howard, and M. J. Boehm Strauss (Eds.), *Everywoman's Guide to Colleges and Universities.* Old Westbury, N.Y.: The Feminist Press, 1982.
Tickton, S. G. *1982 Idea Handbook, Attracting and Retaining Highly Qualified Young Faculty Members at Colleges and Universities.* Washington, D.C.: Academy for Educational Development, 1982.

*Louis F. Brakeman has been provost or dean of the college at Denison University since 1970. He is active in Great Lakes Colleges Association activities. In the summer and fall of 1980, while on leave, he worked on the subject of faculty midcareer renewal.*

*Careful thought and planning will enable a college or university to develop compensation policies that advance institutional goals and objectives.*

# Faculty Compensation Policies

*Fred Silander*

## Goals and Objectives

Colleges and universities exist to accomplish a mission and most such institutions have broad and wide-ranging mission statements. Usually such statements are much too general to serve as guides to action. Consequently, a series of more limited goals or objectives is identified for which specific courses of action are developed.

In order to achieve the desired ends or goals, the institution marshals and manages resources such as labor, material, and finances. Each of these must be managed efficiently and effectively in order to achieve the desired goals. Labor, particularly faculty, is the key ingredient in accomplishing the goals of an academic institution.

Faculty members need to be motivated to perform those functions that enable the institution to achieve its ends. The manner in which compensation influences faculty remains an open question, but it is clear that compensation is an important factor in recruiting and retaining faculty. Activities performed by the faculty are more directly related to the purposes of the college or university than those of any other group. Indeed, one might say that all other activities represent support activities for the instructional process. Faculty compensation policy thus is one means by which the institution influences the faculty to work toward institutional goals.

J. W. Fuller (Ed.). *Issues in Faculty Personnel Policies.* New Directions for Higher Education, no. 41. San Francisco: Jossey-Bass, March 1983.

A recent analysis of college and university goals reveals some interesting conclusions. Richman and Farmer (1974) ranked thirty-one goals of American colleges and universities and found that protecting the faculty, undergraduate education, institutional financial support, and faculty benefits and privileges were the four most important (p. 119). When institutions were classified by type, faculty protection ranked first among all except religious-sponsored institutions, at which it ranked second. Faculty benefits and privileges ranked second in state multi-universities and high-prestige private schools and no lower than sixth among other types of colleges and universities (p. 122). The fact that faculty benefits and privileges were ranked fourth overall and second at some institutions suggests the importance of faculty compensation policy.

Faculty compensation policy must be based on some concept or concepts of compensation. Among the broad criteria for compensation are worth, fairness or equity, need, and market measures. It seems quite clear that faculty compensation is based on all four criteria. Worth, while difficult to determine, is involved with evaluation of and compensation based on measures of research, teaching, and service. Fairness or equity is an issue related to compensation based on comparative responsibilities and particularly concerns minorities, women, part-time faculty members, as well as faculty in general. Evidence of need being used as a criterion is found in fringe benefits, such as staff tuition allowances and health insurance. The influence of the market is readily apparent in the differentials which exist among the disciplines.

Compensation policy involves the concepts above but also other characteristics. Compensation policies and programs must meet legal requirements, including those concerning women and minorities. Sound compensation programs need to provide salaries competitive with other, similar institutions, as well as with those in other sectors of the economy. Finally, compensation policies must provide programs that are efficient and cost-effective.

### Definition of Compensation

Compensation includes salary and fringe benefits. Fringe benefits include all other factors that are part of the employment contract, but from a realistic view should include only those with a measurable monetary value. Most commonly included are life insurance, retirement programs and severance pay, disability insurance, health insurance, sick leave and payment, holidays and vacations, personal days, paid rest periods, and some benefits that may be peculiar to colleges and universities, such as staff tuition benefits. The list could go on to include subsidized housing and meals and even to such areas as prestige attached to being employed by particular institutions, but the criterion of having a monetary value and being part of the employment agreement excludes many such items. Surveys have shown, however, that there is little agreement on the exact nature of benefits but rather that each institution has some variations (Martel, 1982).

## Role of Benefits

Fringe benefits carry a number of advantages and distinctions compared to salary. For example, benefits generally are not taxable as income or at times represent deferred income. Life insurance premiums paid for by employers are not taxable income unless the total exceeds certain levels. Employer pension contributions are tax-deferred until retirement, when the tax liability may be reduced due to income and age.

Some fringe benefits may tie individuals to the institution. To the degree that retirement plans are not vested, they may serve to restrict faculty mobility, although the regulations regarding vesting have served to protect employees. The widespread participation in TIAA–CREF has served to enhance mobility, since it is both portable and owned by the faculty member. Staff tuition programs for dependents clearly encourage faculty to remain at an institution with such a benefit.

From an institutional viewpoint, fringe benefits may be less costly than salary in recruiting and holding faculty. The promise of tuition benefits ten or more years in the future may be less expensive than a higher salary that would enable faculty members to accumulate the same amount for their dependents' college costs. Some faculty members attracted by such a benefit may never have eligible dependents. Also, when the benefit is not currently taxable, the value of the benefit to the faculty member is actually greater than the cost to the institution.

Fringe benefits tend to discriminate among faculty members. Life insurance may be more worthwhile to those with dependents than to those without. Social security benefits may also affect individuals in different ways. Tuition benefits are another obvious example. Housing subsidies in various forms, while not generally considered part of compensation, are a benefit that usually favors younger faculty.

Individual faculty members generally want to maximize the present value of the compensation package. Thus, deferred compensation is desirable only if its value sufficiently exceeds the alternative of current payments. Uncertain future payments (such as dependent tuition payments) must be sufficiently attractive to offset their uncertainty. Restrictive benefits may have no value or even a negative value to ineligible faculty members, since they may be a drain on other elements of compensation.

To the individual, compensation in the form of fringe benefits has the disadvantage of inflexibility compared to salary. In most cases such plans tie the individual to a group plan that attempts to meet the needs of not only faculty but staff as well, though at times faculty benefits may differ from those available to others. One solution to this problem has been developed in recent years — the cafeteria approach.

Cafeteria, sometimes referred to as flexible compensation or flexible benefits, enables employees to choose from a range of benefits up to a maximum amount. This enables them to shape their programs to meet their own particular needs. Not only does a flexible benefits plan allow employees to tailor benefits to their current needs, but it also allows them to meet their changing needs. Further, flexible programs may actually increase both the value of such benefits and the appreciation of employees. On the other hand, employees may make poor choices with negative effects on morale. Also, such programs are quite difficult and costly to administer (Rosenbloom and Hallman, 1981, pp. 430–431).

An early concern regarding such plans was the tax treatment of benefits when the employee has a choice between taxable and nontaxable benefits. The Revenue Act of 1978 clarified the situation by providing that such programs will not subject the employee to taxes on ordinarily nontaxable benefits, although any taxable benefits chosen would be considered part of gross income for tax purposes (Rosenbloom and Hallman, 1981, p. 457).

The distribution of compensation between salary and various benefits is an issue for both the institution and the faculty member. The institution must consider the compensation package in recruiting and retaining the types of individuals it desires. If, for example, a university wishes to attract extremely promising faculty members for relatively short periods (such as three years), it may wish to emphasize the salary component of compensation. Conversely, a desire to build a stable faculty suggests elements of compensation that require faculty to commit themselves to the university for a lengthy period. There is evidence that some benefits (retirement) decrease mobility, while others (medical and life insurance) appear to have little effect (Mitchell, 1982, p. 297). Consequently, institutional policy regarding the nature, as well as the amount, of compensation depends on institutional goals and objectives.

Benefit programs involve large expenditures and are very important in maintaining a faculty; consequently, careful planning is essential. Past practices of allowing benefits packages to develop haphazardly are no longer acceptable. Because of the importance of benefit programs, a number of institutions employ consultants to assist them in such planning.

Acceptance of even the finest benefit package requires faculty participation in its development. Effective and continuing communication with the faculty concerning existing and new benefits, costs, and potential changes is essential.

## What Is Happening to Compensation?

In its "Annual Report on the Economic Status of the Profession, 1981–82" ("Annual Report...," 1982), the AAUP indicated that in 1981–82 salaries for faculty across all types of colleges and universities underwent a 9 percent increase, which, in light of an 8.7 percent rate of inflation, resulted in increased real income for the first time since the 1960s (p. 3). The 1981–82 salary increases were greatest in Category I institutions (9.4 percent), with smaller increases for Categories IIA (8.4 percent), IIB (8.9 percent), and III (8.5 percent) (p. 14).

Despite the modest increase in real income during the past year, over a longer period faculty members have suffered significant losses of real income — 20.7 percent during the past ten years and 12.8 percent since 1975–76 (p. 5).

Fringe benefits have been increasing more rapidly than salary in recent years, causing total compensation to rise by 10.1 percent. In 1969–70 benefits were 10.6 percent of salaries but by 1978–79 had reached 17.5 percent and by 1981–82 were 19.3 percent of salary (Hansen, 1981, p. 8). These changes represent primarily increases in mandated benefits, such as Social Security and unemployment and workmens compensation, but they may also reflect policies placing greater emphasis on benefits ("Annual Report," 1982, p. 4). These increases in benefits still leave faculty far behind workers in business and industry, where benefits range from 25 to 40 percent of salary (Hansen, 1981, p. 8).

## Issues in Compensation

*Structure of Compensation.* A wide variety of differentials in compensation exist. Male faculty members are reputed to be paid more than their female counterparts. Research faculty are often treated differently from those who are primarily teachers. Faculty members who publish do better than those who do not. Degrees also make a difference. Race undoubtedly matters. Administrators need to examine such differentials in their organizations to determine whether they are appropriate and consistent with organizational goals.

Tuckman and Tuckman (1976) conducted an analysis of salary differences among faculty and came to a variety of conclusions. They found that those who publish articles earn more than those who do not and that the level of earnings is greater for those with more publications. This conclusion is not surprising, but what may be is the finding that publishing articles is more remunerative than publishing books. Research is apparently valued more highly than teaching, perhaps because research is more highly valued in the large and prestigious institutions and because it is easier to evaluate. Also, faculty members who participate in administration earn more than those who are limited to academic activities. It appears that black faculty members are compensated more highly than their white counterparts. The authors indicate that the differential is probably due to affirmative action and equal opportunity efforts, the limited number of blacks available in the market, and the large nonacademic demand that exists.

Another structural compensation issue is the relationship between educational and noneducational salaries. In order to attract and retain capable young faculty it is important to maintain salaries comparable with those in the private and governmental sectors. On the other hand, an excess of new Ph.D.s over faculty openings would logically lead to a decline in faculty salaries relative to those in the public and private sectors. Just such an excess has existed in the 1970s and is expected to continue on a reduced scale until the 1990s.

A review of the past ten years indicates faculty in general have not fared as well as comparable professional and technical groups in the private sector. Attorneys, engineers, chemists, personnel directors, and buyers have all done better in real terms than college faculty members. Federal government employees have fared about as well (or poorly) as faculty members ("Annual Report...," 1982, p. 7).

Administrators are continually vexed by the need to attract faculty members in all disciplines and to maintain reasonable salary differentials between the disciplines on campus. Excessive spreads raise questions of equity and may lead to dissatisfaction. What has been happening to relative salaries among the disciplines? Between 1976–77 and 1981–82 the average salaries of new assistant professors in the fields of business, computer information, and engineering rose by 53 percent, 64 percent, and 58 percent, respectively, compared to increases of 32 percent in interdisciplinary studies and letters, 30 percent in foreign languages, and 44 percent for all disciplines ("Annual Report...," 1982, p. 9). It appears that strong enrollment pressure and demand from the nonacademic areas have caused computer, business, and engineering faculty salaries to rise substantially more than those in other areas. The combination of growth in some areas and decline in others has caused the spread from highest to lowest salaries among disciplines to increase. The ratio of the spread between disciplines with the highest and lowest salaries among assistant professors was 1.67 compared to 1.49 for full professors in the same disciplines (p. 9). Unless university administrations can make equity adjustments in the next several years or market conditions change significantly, the issue of salary spreads between the disciplines will be heightened. Obviously, this is a matter that will require close attention during the next five to ten years. Even as reality forces us to accept some salary differences based on the different market demand for faculty in various disciplines, it is important to monitor those differences to be sure they do not persist after market conditions to justify them have changed. There is far less difference in the market value of faculty members after fifteen or twenty years of teaching than among those fresh from graduate training.

Differentials of other types exist partly as a matter of university policy, partly due to circumstances. Women, for example, tend to be paid less than men largely due to historical reasons, some of which undoubtedly were matters of policy.

The AAUP data show that women's salaries are lower than those of men, but the data must be examined carefully. Comparison of men's and women's salaries by rank or type of institution are difficult because women tend to be found in larger proportions in the lower-paying classifications of institutions and in the lower ranks. Comparison by ranks by type of institution does indicate lower salaries for women ("Annual Report...," 1982, p. 4). Even this comparison is unreliable because it fails to consider factors such as experience, productivity, and academic discipline.

A number of studies have been conducted to account for these other factors and to determine whether differences in salaries between men and women do exist. Tuckman's study (1976) suggests that when one examines differences in men's and women's salaries relative to publications of books, public service, and administration, women are paid less than men with similar skills, while degree of teaching skill does not appear to make a difference in salaries. However, those women who publish articles earn more than men who publish articles. When comparing male and female teachers with no teaching awards, no publications, and no public service or administrative experience, starting salaries for women were found to be higher than those for men. However, after the first few years of experience, salaries for men begin to exceed those of women (pp. 60–61). Several studies cited by Koch (1982) indicate that women faculty members earn less than men with similar qualifications. One of these studies (Tuckman and Tuckman, 1976) indicated a number of reasons for the differentials, including lack of research opportunities, heavy teaching and advising loads, lack of support for scholarly work, and less mobility than male faculty members. These differentials are likely to diminish over time because better academic job opportunities are being offered women and many institutions are making equity adjustments.

Compensation differs among the various groups within institutions—faculty, administration, and staff—as well as among the faculty members themselves. The disparity among the groups is a matter of concern, since individuals do appear to respond when excessive differentials exist. A recent study of blue-collar workers concluded that "people do detect upward dissimilar pay comparisons" (Martin, 1982, p. 120). When a group of employees does note significant differences between its earnings and those of a dissimilar group, the result can lead to serious dissatisfaction. There is no reason to assume that faculty members do not respond in a similar way in relation to other groups such as administrators.

Salary structures do present administrators with a complex set of differential salaries that must be effectively managed. Some of these differentials are the result of market conditions, some are due to differences in background, while others may represent discrimination in favor of some at the expense of others. Some differentials are permissible legally; others are not. Some may result in inequities. A number of institutions are attempting to identify the differentials and determine if inequities exist.

Three basic techniques for analyzing salary structure have been employed. The first, job evaluation, involves identifying the elements of the job for which compensation would be made and to which points are assigned. The second pairs two faculty members with similar backgrounds and compares their salaries. Difficulties with these relatively simple techniques have led to the use of the more complex multiple-regression analysis. This procedure involves the use of quantitative estimates of the influence of numerous variables on salaries and produces predicted salaries that can be compared with actual salaries. Koch (1982) discusses the various techniques and Pezzullo and Brittingham (1979) provide a series of articles and case studies on the use of multiple regression in determining salary equity.

Whatever techniques are used for identifying the salary structure, once differentials are measured, it then becomes a matter of policy to examine and deal with them. Many, if not most, of the differences are legitimate and appropriate but some require adjustments for reasons of equity. Birnbaum (1979, p. 142) suggests that when making equity adjustments, raises should be made on the basis of both merit and the equity differential.

*Merit.* Merit pay systems are designed to motivate individuals to be more productive. Such systems involve monetary incentives tied to some measure of performance and are based on the assumption that individuals will respond to those incentives. Effective incentive pay systems must provide clearly understood criteria for measuring output, established standards of performance, and a recognition by employees that they can improve performance and that such improvement will lead to a higher level of pay.

The concept of merit pay has generally been accepted in business and industry, although even there it is coming under considerable scrutiny and criticism. Early approaches to productivity tended to view the worker as another machine and ignored the human side of work. Particularly since the 1930s, the emphasis has changed toward increased concern for the employees and their attitudes. Indeed, the attitudes of workers themselves have changed over the years. As basic needs have been met, higher-level needs have become more important so that the workers' emphasis has changed from pay to working conditions, self-fulfillment, and personal growth.

Does pay motivate employees toward higher levels of productivity? Many workers would answer affirmatively, but studies indicate that fairness of the pay is also a significant factor in morale and satisfaction. Also, benefits may be more important to some than the salary itself by providing, for example, sick leave and more leisure time through longer vacations (Bass and Barrett, 1981, p. 107). Further, the manner in which the pay or salary is determined may be as or more important than the amount itself. It is important that the salary be perceived to be what the employee feels it should be and that the pay criteria be appropriate, accurately measured, understood by the employee, and adhered to by management (Dyer and Theriault, 1976, pp. 602–603).

Why is merit a consideration in the college and university setting? While merit has been an internally imposed constraint in business, boards and state legislatures have placed emphasis on merit in educational institutions. If merit salary systems are to be employed they should improve performance in the areas of research, teaching, and service, and maintain and improve faculty morale.

If merit compensation is to improve productivity, then there must be an acceptable system for evaluating teaching, scholarship, and service. It is not self-evident that the use of merit for salary purposes is appropriate, but if it is to be successful, adequate evaluation of the three performance areas must be possible.

Even when evaluation of a college or university teacher's performance is appropriate and accepted by the faculty member, and the connection between pay and performance is recognized, does it mean merit pay systems are an effective means of improving productivity? Reference to the general literature on employee motivation seems to indicate that other elements play a major role in faculty productivity and that pay is not a primary motivator (Bass and Barrett, 1981; Hackman, Lawler, and Porter, 1977; Shultz, 1982). There is also some concern expressed in the literature that merit pay systems for faculty may not even be effective (Miller and Young, 1979, p. 8). Another source indicates that trust, working conditions, and institutional identification contribute to faculty well-being and, in all probability, productivity, but that compensation is only one among a myriad of factors in morale (Baldridge and others, 1978). On the other hand, an extensive study by Howard Tuckman (1976) of the reward system concludes that evaluation systems can be developed and that more rewards should be offered for teaching and service activities. The study lends support to the idea that an appropriate evaluation and reward system can be developed that will affect the behavior of faculty members (p. 17).

If merit compensation is difficult and perhaps not even feasible, what are the alternatives? Salary schedules based on rank and time in rank tend to predominate. Entry salary becomes significant because it is the base from which subsequent increases are calculated. Salary increases may be stated in absolute or percentage terms, either across the board or by ranks. Absolute increases, especially when equal across ranks, tend to prevent dollar differentials from rising. Percentage increases, unless inversely related to rank, cause the spread to widen significantly over time.

Wide spreads in compensation may be more acceptable in some situations than others. Universities that are clearly seen to reward the nationally known, well-published scholars appear to manage wide differentials without creating unacceptable morale problems. Other colleges and universities, perhaps the majority, must seriously consider the impact of a wide range from highest to lowest salaries. Industrial and personnel psychologists indicate that for pay to be satisfactory it must be perceived to be appropriate, among other things, in terms of the salary received by others performing in a similar manner (Bass and Barrett, 1981, p. 112). Since faculty in primarily teaching institutions see each other as doing essentially the same kinds of things, the salary range becomes important in determining faculty morale.

The effectiveness of merit pay remains uncertain. The general literature on motivation appears to be moving away from pay as a significant motivator, although monetary incentives continue to be employed widely in business and industry. Many colleges and universities use various incentive programs for rewarding scholarly efforts as well as teaching. In order to have a chance at being successful, such programs must be carefully developed along guidelines found in the employee motivation literature.

*Pay for Other Activities.* The level of faculty salaries in relation to inflation and salaries in noneducational pursuits raises the issue of supplementary compensation. Some faculty are able to generate additional income through grants and research projects while others supplement their incomes through consulting. However, many faculty members are unable to utilize those or other resources to augment their incomes. Universities frequently have available opportunities for additional income in the form of overload or summer teaching and research and occasional administrative responsibilities.

Overload teaching is usually compensated at less than pro rata rates since teaching is only a portion of the faculty member's total responsibility. Summer school rates vary among institutions from a fraction of pro rata to full pro rata amounts. Compensation for administrative duties such as department chairmanships is usually nominal but must be sufficiently attractive to compensate for the efforts required. At times, department chairmen have received a higher salary for accepting the responsibilities involved while in other institutions a separate stipend is paid. The latter arrangement is more appropriate when chairmanships are designed to change relatively often since the other procedure leads to building in compensation when those positions turn over. A similar situation exists for athletic directors and coaches who may remain at an institution after having been relieved of those responsibilities. It appears to be advantageous to compensate separately for such activities since it greatly simplifies salary determination when such changes do occur. The AAUP salary study indicates that faculty members, on the average, earn about one additional month's salary. Such earnings, however, are likely to be rather uncertain from year to year ("Annual Report...," 1982, p. 5).

*Part-Time Instruction.* One of the most troublesome areas of compensation policy is that involving part-time teachers. The matter involves the entire range of compensation questions as well as issues of tenure and promotion.

Part-time instructors make up about 30 percent of total faculty personnel but that ratio is expected, according to one study, to rise to

40 percent by 1985 (Leslie, Kellams, and Gunne, 1982, pp. 18, 34). The same study indicates part-time faculty are used most heavily in two-year colleges and in colleges which are rapidly expanding, in newly developing programs, and where there is an emphasis on teaching loads with few other responsibilities.

There are several categories of part-time teachers. For some their earnings are additions to full-time income. On the other hand, as many as 30 percent of part-time faculty teach part-time because full-time positions are not available to them (Stern and others, 1981, p. 36). The remainder is made up of students, retirees, or those with no other part- or full-time employment.

Salary is perhaps the prime concern and involves a number of issues. Procedures for determining salaries vary widely from a single salary level for all part-time instructors to very complicated schedules involving years of experience, time taught at the institution, and degrees. Some universities apply a system of ranks to part-time faculty along the same lines as for regular faculty. Frequently it is necessary to make salary allowances by discipline, just as is done for full-time faculty, since it may be equally difficult, for example, to attract part- and full-time computer science teachers. There also may be differentials between academic and nonacademic part-time instructors. Business and other professionals are frequently employed on a part-time basis and in many instances may be willing to teach largely for the prestige of being associated with a college or university. The entire part-time rate schedule may be affected by the supply of nonacademic personnel.

The study by Leslie, Kellams, and Gunne (1982, p. 78) indicates that part-time salaries prorated against full-time salaries are not common. The obvious reason is that full-time teachers do more than teach whereas normally part-timers are limited to teaching. Often schools will attempt to determine what fraction of full-time faculty efforts go into teaching and then calculate a per-course rate for teaching only. The full-time salary level used for such a calculation is often a rather low base salary.

The full range of fringe benefits is not usually provided for part-time faculty members. The issues regarding benefits involve both equity and cost considerations. Benefits are limited because of costs and also because of the difficulties of administration. Benefits based on salary (such as retirement contributions) are simple enough to administer, but others such as life and health insurance create problems of coverage periods and proportion.

The February/March 1981 issue of *Academe* presents an excellent discussion of the entire range of issues involving part-time faculty.

One of several recommendations in the report states "that the part-time faculty member whose contribution to the academic program of the institution and to its academic life is equal to that of a full-timer except for the proportion of time given to the position, and whose qualifications are comparable, receive prorated compensation" (p. 37). Similar recommendations are made for the extension of fringe benefits with further recommendations that benefits be available to all part-time faculty members.

The legal issues of part-time faculty are carefully addressed by Leslie, Kellams, and Gunne (1982, pp. 47–71). They deal with both constitutional issues (due process and equal protection) and statutory coverage as well as legal questions arising from collective bargaining arrangements. An important conclusion they reach concerning legal issues is that "terms and conditions of employment must be carefully stated and classified" (p. 71).

All administrators would do well to examine their procedures for hiring and compensating part-time faculty. The issue will continue to receive attention from both full- and part-time faculty as well as from administrators.

*Effects of Inflation.* Inflation has clearly wreaked havoc on the real income of faculty members, one measure of the havoc being the 12.8 percent decline in real income incurred during the last five years. While all faculty members have been affected, the economic impact on new assistant professors perhaps has been the sharpest. According to the AAUP report, the Consumer Price Index rose by nearly 60 percent from 1976 to 1981 while the salaries of new assistant professors rose by 44 percent. However certain faculty groups such as those in business, computer information, and engineering had increases significantly larger than the average. The salaries of beginning faculty members in thirteen of twenty-two disciplines rose by less than 40 percent, averaging about 35 percent, with several rising by only 30 to 34 percent, whereas among full professors only six disciplines had increases of less than 40 percent. In fourteen of the twenty-two disciplines salaries of new assistant professors rose by smaller percentages than did salaries of already higher-paid full professors ("Annual Report...," 1982, pp. 8–9). Clearly, the real income of new assistant professors in most disciplines declined significantly more than that of senior faculty.

This situation has led to financial difficulties for young faculty and perhaps some concerns about salary equity among the ranks. One indication of the financial problems facing young faculty is the difficulty many have in purchasing homes. Beginning salaries of $17,000 to $19,000 do not make young assistant professors prime candidates for mortgage loans in markets where interest rates range upward from 14 percent. In response college and university administrations have considered or adopted various plans to help young faculty acquire housing. These range from subsidized rentals in university-owned housing to subsidized first or second mortgages. Whatever the forms and areas of assistance offered, they are but recognition of the financial difficulties created by the high rates of inflation on the economic condition of new faculty.

Obviously, double-digit or near double-digit inflation has had an impact on all faculty and has created pressures on the institution to provide salary adjustments at levels that at least maintain real incomes. This, in turn, puts pressure on the university to generate sufficient income from tuition, endowment, or governmental sources to meet those needs.

The recent abatement in the inflation rate will reduce pressures on salaries of all faculty members, but the impact of the past inflation on the purchasing power of current salaries still remains. The inflation rate has an effect on a variety of administrative decisions, not the least of which are decisions involving compensation.

## Summary

Faculty compensation represents perhaps the single largest operating expenditure colleges and universities make, and on the basis of size alone, compensation requires careful attention. Beyond that, the level and structure of compensation is likely to affect faculty attitudes and influence their behavior. As a result, compensation policy becomes a very significant issue and needs to be carefully developed to achieve the goals of the college or university.

Compensation includes both salary and benefits. The wide range of available benefits presents the institution with the opportunity to meet the needs of faculty, although it is difficult to meet everyone's individual desires. A flexible benefits program can be tailored to personal needs but is quite difficult to administer.

During both the past five to ten years faculty compensation has fallen behind increases in the cost of living. Benefits have increased faster than salary, increasing from 10.6 to 19.3 percent of salary since 1969–70.

A number of issues arise in determining compensation. What premiums are to be paid for those who publish or do significant research or participate in administrative work? How should faculty salaries compare with nonacademic pay? Are differentials among disciplines appropriate and, if so, to what extent? Are women paid less, and, if so, is the situation equitable? These and other causes for differentials in the structure of compensation exist, and it is important for administrators to use available techniques for identifying and then dealing with them.

Merit pay has been popular in business and industry, and has been utilized in determining faculty compensation. Recent research in motivation leans away from the earlier position and stresses the manner in which compensation is determined as well as other noncompensation factors in determining productivity and morale.

Part-time instruction is becoming more important at many institutions and those faculty members generally are compensated less well on a relative basis than full-time faculty. Careful planning is required to avoid inequities and exploitation in compensation for this particular group of faculty members.

Other issues that need to be recognized are compensation for other activities and the effects of inflation on all faculty members but particularly on the younger faculty.

The long list of complex issues in compensation creates problems in determining appropriate compensation policies, but the importance of the entire matter calls for compensation policy planning at the highest levels.

## References

"Annual Report on the Economic Status of the Profession, 1981–82." *Academe,* 1982, *68* (4), 1–78.

Baldridge, J. V., Curtis, D. V., Ecker, G., and Riley, G. L. *Policy Making and Effective Leadership.* San Francisco: Jossey-Bass, 1978.

Bass, B. M., and Barrett, G. V. *People, Work, and Organizations: An Introduction to Industrial and Organizational Psychology.* Boston: Allyn & Bacon, 1981.

Birnbaum, M. H. "Procedures for the Determination and Correction of Salary Inequities." In T. R. Pezzullo and B. E. Brittingham (Eds.), *Salary Equity: Detecting Sex Bias in Salary Among College and University Professors.* Lexington, Mass.: Heath, 1979.

Dyer, L., and Theriault, R. "Determinants of Pay Satisfaction." *Journal of Applied Psychology,* 1976, *61* (5), 596–604.

Hackman, J. R., Lawler, E. E., and Porter, L. W. *Perspectives on Behavior in Organizations.* New York: McGraw-Hill, 1977.

Hansen, W. L. "The Decline of Real Faculty Salaries in the 1970s." *Quarterly Review of Economics and Business,* 1981, *21* (4), 7–12.

Koch, J. V. "Salary Equity Issues in Higher Education: Where Do We Stand?" *AAHE Bulletin,* October 1982, 7–14.

Leslie, D. W., Kellams, S. E., and Gunne, G. M. *Part-Time Faculty in American Higher Education.* New York: Praeger, 1982.

Martel, P. "A Model of Total Compensation in a Market Comparability Framework." *Public Personnel Management Journal,* 1982, *11* (2), 148–156.

Martin, J. "The Fairness of Earnings Differentials: An Experimental Study of Blue Collar Workers." *Journal of Human Resources,* 1982, *17* (1), 110–122.

36

Miller, J. R., and Young, J. I. "Merit Pay: An Unexamined Concept in Higher Education." *The Journal of the College and University Personnel Association,* 1979, *30* (4), 7–14.

Mitchell, O. S. "Fringe Benefits and Labor Mobility." *Journal of Human Resources,* 1982, *17* (2), 286–298.

Pezzullo, T. R., and Brittingham, B. E. *Salary Equity: Detecting Sex Bias in Salary Among College and University Professors.* Lexington, Mass.: Heath, 1979.

Richman, B. M., and Farmer, R. N. *Leadership, Goals, and Power in Higher Education.* San Francisco: Jossey-Bass, 1974.

Rosenbloom, J. S., and Hallman, G. V. *Employee Benefit Planning.* Englewood Cliffs, N.J.: Prentice-Hall, 1981.

Schultz, D. P. *Psychology and Industry Today: An Introduction to Industrial and Organizational Psychology,* 3rd ed. New York: Macmillan, 1982.

Stern, C. S., and others. "The Status of Part-Time Faculty." *Academe,* 1981, *67* (1), 29–39.

Tuckman, H. P. *Publication, Teaching and the Academic Reward Structure.* Lexington, Mass.: Heath, 1976.

Tuckman, H. P., and Tuckman, B. "Structure of Salaries at American Universities." *Journal of Higher Education,* 1976, *47* (January), 51–64.

*Fred Silander is vice-president for finance and professor of economics and management at DePauw University, where he previously served as dean of the faculty.*

*While the explosion of knowledge and decline of faculty morale*
*both plead for more frequent leaves and fewer restrictions upon*
*them, hard times in the academy make liberalization of*
*current leave policies highly unlikely.*

# Faculty Leaves

## David G. Marker

The regular practice of granting leaves to faculty of universities and
colleges in order to "freshen and add new stimulus to their work" began
to gain prominence in America in this century. The *Cyclopedia of Education* reported:

> By an ancient law the Israelites were commanded every seventh
> year, "the sabbatical year" to suffer their fields and vineyards to
> rest or to lie untilled. The term sabbatical year is now widely
> used among colleges and universities to mean an intermission of
> labor, first for rest or pleasure, or second for research or study
> uninterrupted by teaching. The value of granting leaves of
> absence to teachers in order to freshen and to add new stimulus
> to their work is heartily conceded by educators. The practice
> each year is being extended as colleges gain in financial strength
> and the provisions under which college teachers are able to take
> such intermission from their work are becoming more and more
> definitely formulated ["Sabbatical Year...," 1912, p. 540]

In the years following, other types of leaves have become
common in the academy. The purposes of these leaves include such
diverse objectives as professional development, degree completion,
teaching at another institution, career reassessment, and childrearing.

J. W. Fuller (Ed.). *Issues in Faculty Personnel Policies.* New Directions for
Higher Education, no. 41. San Francisco: Jossey-Bass, March 1983.

While the policies and practices governing leaves of various kinds differ from institution to institution, they have many features in common. The following description and analysis is based upon an examination of the leave policies of twenty-five distinguished liberal arts colleges: the twelve members of the Great Lakes Colleges Association (GLCA) and the thirteen colleges of the Associated Colleges of the Midwest (ACM) (Great Lakes..., 1980). In addition to an examination of the leave policies themselves, questionnaires on current conventions and trends involving leaves were sent to the chief academic officers of approximately one-half of these colleges. General comments on leaves were solicited from all chief academic officers (also referred to hereafter as deans) in ACM and GLCA; some were received in writing, others arose in personal conversations.

## General Features of Sabbatical Leave Policies

*Purpose.* College policies generally state or imply that sabbatical leaves are intended primarily for the improvement of teaching, for course development, and for scholarly or artistic work that will contribute to the intellectual and professional growth of faculty members.

A great majority of the policies state unambiguously that sabbaticals are intended to benefit the college, and its students as well, through the professional development of faculty as teachers and scholars. This expectation is reflected further in the policies by the requirement that faculty return to full-time teaching at the conclusion of a sabbatical leave, usually for at least one year. At some colleges where sabbaticals may be taken more frequently than once in seven years, the time back may be equal to the leave period. Presumably, the rationale for this requirement is that the colleges provide compensation during the sabbatical not only for the professional development and personal refreshment of faculty but also so that students can benefit from the intellectual and psychic renewal that faculty members gain while on leave. (Policies seem not to mention "rest or pleasure" as does the paragraph quoted from the *Cyclopedia of Education*!) Based upon the same rationale, some leave policies contain the proviso that a faculty member may not apply for sabbatical if he or she is within several terms of retirement.

Exceptions to the generally agreed-upon and relatively narrow purposes of sabbaticals are found in a small (but slowly increasing) number of colleges. Denison University, for example, allows sabbaticals that "permit the utilization of special expertise of faculty in programs of broad interests (such as programs sponsored by professional societies or by the federal government)" and "permits experiences in other nonacademic settings that hold promise in developing new competencies and provide opportunities to test out alternative careers" (Brakeman, 1980). While it is possible to argue that the first of these may well contribute to the professional development and stature of the faculty member through service, the latter explicitly allows for leaves that enable a faculty member to test alternative careers and thereby potentially to leave the college and/or the academy. Ohio Wesleyan does not exclude the possibilities that the Denison policy states explicitly. In the past few years, Albion has approved leaves for nontraditional purposes that could lead to career changes.

*Frequency.* In colleges with a semester calendar, the most common practice is to allow a leave of one or two semesters in every seven years (commonly in the seventh year following six years of full-time service).

In colleges on term calendars, it is often possible to apply for a leave of one term more frequently than every seventh year. At Ohio Wesleyan University, for example, a faculty member is eligible for a one-term leave with pay during every fourth year.

It is interesting to note a new program being instituted at Monmouth College in 1983–84 in which a faculty member is eligible for a one-term "sabbatical" leave every three and one-third years (Monmouth is on a three-term calendar). The new policy states that faculty are "expected to take a sabbatical every tenth term" (Amy, 1982).

More usually, however, eligibility for a sabbatical occurs once every seven years, as the name implies.

*Compensation.* Those on sabbatical leave commonly receive one semester's salary for a leave of one or two semesters. Hence, for a one-semester leave the faculty member receives full salary during the leave period; for a two-semester leave, he or she receives one-half of the normal salary for the leave period. While relatively few policies explicitly state that fringe benefits are paid during the leave the implication is that all benefits continue as if the faculty member were on campus. Possible exceptions are those benefits that normally are computed and paid as a percentage of the faculty member's salary (such as contributions to a retirement plan). If a person on leave is receiving one-half or three-fourths of regular salary, the benefit may be either that percentage of the amount actually being paid or the same amount a faculty member would receive if on campus and being paid full salary.

Generally, the colleges encourage faculty members, especially those who wish to take a full year's leave at partial salary, to obtain additional funding from outside sources. Primary sources have been governmental agencies and private and public foundations. Examples include the National Science Foundation (NSF), the National Endowment for the Humanities (NEH), and the Fulbright and Woodrow Wilson Fellowship Programs. If a faculty member is able to obtain additional funding from any such source, most policies state that the total compensation—including salary and benefits—he or she receives while on leave may not exceed the total compensation that would be received if on campus.

A number of chief academic officers perceive that there is increasing difficulty in obtaining supplemental funding from outside sources for this purpose. One dean reported that, in his experience, increased difficulty is particularly evident in the humanities. Another believes that more ingenuity and effort are required to obtain grants than were true a decade ago.

In contrast to the perception of many deans, Ida Wallace, director of the Independent Colleges Office in Washington, reports that "federal grants still exist to provide support to leave recipients" (Wallace, 1982). In fact, with the exception of NSF Faculty Fellowships, Ms. Wallace estimates that there have been substantial gains in the number of federal funding sources. She cites as examples: NEH Fellowships for College Teachers, more small grants from NIH, more National Academy of Science/National Research Council Associateships in government laboratories, grants from the National Endowment for the Arts, and summer grants from NEH and NASA.

The perception that supplemental funding is more difficult to obtain, or is completely unavailable, may discourage some faculty from applying when making leave plans. It is important for deans and departmental chairpersons to remain current about funding possibilities, and to encourage faculty to apply for support well in advance of the planned leave.

*Institutional Investment or Faculty Right?* As mentioned above, virtually every sabbatical leave policy either states explicitly or implies that sabbatical leaves are for the benefit of faculty *and* their colleges. A proposal in which the faculty member outlines detailed plans for a leave is required by almost every college; in only a few is the applicant required simply to notify the dean that he or she will be on leave. Similarly, almost every college requires a written report at the conclusion of the leave.

Several policies are of special interest because they represent extrema. Beloit's policy states that the college "*expects* every member to apply and qualify for such a leave once in every seven years" (Wong, 1982). Emphasizing the importance of qualifying, however, the statement also says that "the proposed project to be carried out under the leave must constitute genuine scholarly development and is to be attested to by professional colleagues in the applicant's department and, when necessary, by professional colleagues from outside [the college]."

In contrast to Beloit's statement, an Ohio Wesleyan faculty member need only notify the dean that he or she intends to go on leave; a formal proposal is not required.

An overwhelming majority of the policy statements and comments from chief academic officers suggest that in the twenty-five colleges whose policies were examined, a sabbatical leave is considered an institutional investment rather than a right.

*Leave Replacements.* Many leave policy statements explicitly state that the department from which the applicant comes must make arrangements, whenever possible, to cover the faculty member's responsibilities while he or she is on leave. This is not always possible, especially in departments with a small number of faculty or when the faculty member normally teaches a critical course which cannot be canceled during the leave period.

Given the state of the economy and the projected student enrollments in all academic institutions in the decade ahead, the requirement of "no replacement" is likely to be enforced even more rigorously in the future than it has been in the past. Departments will need to be more creative in finding ways to cover, and more careful coordination of leaves likely will be necessary.

*Special Features.* Many policies explicitly forbid a faculty member from engaging in gainful employment while on sabbatical leave. This is especially true if the home institution is paying full salary and benefits; it is less likely to be true if a person is being paid only a fractional salary. Historically, faculty members have been encouraged to obtain supplemental support from foundations or other agencies to assist in funding leaves. Part-time teaching while on leave is discouraged; given special circumstances, it may be allowed occasionally.

Many colleges impose a limit either by department or across the college on the number of persons in any one semester or term that may be on leave. While these limits may be related to financial constraints, they are also imposed in the interests of maintaining continuity of the educational program.

Policy statements often urge faculty members to absent themselves from the college community during the leave period. Two-thirds of the deans polled by written questionnaire responded that more faculty members are spending their sabbaticals and other leaves "in town." Several deans gave virtually identical responses when asked to comment on the result of this practice. As one expressed it: "the biggest problem is making the decision to divorce oneself psychologically and physically from campus activities to enable full focus on the leave activities" (Board, 1980). Three other deans polled believe that in-town leaves are not as productive as those taken out of town. One remarked that "the ['in-town'] leave is less than a leave; time spent is too often in unproductive, familiar behavior" (Irish, 1980). Another indicated that he believed in-town leaves are a mistake; he and departmental chairpersons encourage faculty to leave town with the result that "most do, a few don't" (Powell, 1980).

In order to better understand the reasons for an increasing number of in-town leaves, one of the survey questions was: Are the constraints of family responsibilities and/or of the spouse's career a problem for a significant number of faculty?

Three-quarters of the deans to whom the survey was addressed answered this question affirmatively. In their comments, they suggested that the constraints named in the question make it more difficult for a faculty member to get away from town and campus for an extended period. As a result, the number of requests for year-long leaves has been reduced with a corresponding increase in number of requests for on-campus or in-town sabbaticals.

**Leaves of Absence**

Generally a faculty member may obtain a leave of absence, without pay, to enable the fulfillment of professional or personal objectives. Such leaves may be referred to also as unfunded, unpaid, or unsalaried. Many leave policies state or imply that the objectives of such leaves may be considerably broader than those of sabbaticals.

Leaves of absence generally may be taken at times when they can be conveniently worked into the teaching schedule of the department in which the faculty member resides. He or she does not receive any salary while on a leave of absence, although special arrangements, which differ widely from college to college, are usually possible that enable the continuation of fringe benefits. While a brief application stating the objectives of the leave is usually required, a final report is not common. Limitations on work for gainful employment during the leave period and whether the leave is to be in town or out of town are apparently not thought to be relevant to the granting of this type of leave.

**Special Leaves**

A number of colleges have at least one additional type of leave, some of which are cited in the following examples. At Kalamazoo "any faculty member may apply to receive a leave of one or more quarters at full pay" (Board, 1980). These developmental leaves are ordinarily "granted for purposes which relate to particular program objectives, such as the development of a new course, revision of the curriculum, or acquisition of specific skills such as in counseling." Oberlin faculty "may apply for 'sabbatical' leaves after four or five years of teaching following their initial appointment or following their last sabbatical leave. These leaves will be considered only after regular sabbatical leaves have been evaluated (by the appropriate faculty committee)" (Longsworth, 1980). The purpose of an *early sabbatical* is the same as for a regular one. The College of Wooster awards a *study leave* of one quarter after six quarters of teaching and a leave of three quarters after eighteen quarters of teaching. A full or associate professor is eligible for a *research leave* of three quarters after twelve quarters of teaching or for a leave of one quarter after five quarters of teaching. An assistant professor or instructor is eligible for a research leave of three quarters after fifteen quarters of teaching at Wooster or for a leave of one quarter after six quarters of teaching. Each year Antioch awards "a small number (no more than two or three per year) of special award leaves up to a full year with pay" (Goldberg, 1980). In addition to the usual sabbatical options (one or two semesters every seven years), Denison awards some one-semester leaves after only six semesters of full-time teaching since the previous sabbatical. The compensation for the year in which such a leave is taken is three-fourths of the annual rate.

While these examples do not exhaust the types of special leaves, they give some indication of the diversity of "other" leaves that have been devised to meet the needs of institutions and their faculties.

## Changing Leave Policies in Light of Changing Needs

A number of currently existing factors are conspiring to make changes in leave policies important for the continued vitality of colleges and universities in the several decades ahead. One dean stated his belief in the importance of leaves in the future as follows: "I think leave programs are crucial to preserve because of limited faculty mobility and turnover and the 'greying' of present faculties" (Wong, 1982). The body of knowledge in certain fields, such as computer science and the physical sciences, approximately doubles in each decade. More frequent leaves would be helpful, especially in these fields, to keep faculty at the cutting edge. It is no longer generally true that colleges are gaining in financial strength as they were in 1912 ("Sabbatical Year...," 1912, p. 240). This creates pressures to contract or hold steady the presently available leave opportunities.

Little evidence needs to be supplied to convince the reader of the severe limits imposed on faculty mobility in the last fifteen years with the resulting effects on faculty morale. It is interesting to note that Richard Bolles' book, *What Color Is Your Parachute?*, which is aimed at job-hunters and career changers, has appeared frequently in the survey, "What They're Reading on College Campuses." The popularity of Bolles' book among academics suggests that leave policies, which make it respectable and possible to use sabbaticals to explore new career alternatives, may constitute one important way to deal with this challenge. At the same time, such a solution also may make it possible for newly prepared persons to enter the profession. (Roger Baldwin discusses this issue more fully in a later chapter in this volume.)

Many of the policies make it impossible for a faculty member to take a leave within one or two years of retirement. Because a sabbatical might be useful to a faculty member in preparing for retirement, consideration should be given to the elimination of this requirement.

How realistic are these proposals? Are leaves currently being utilized for such purposes? To gain some insight into the answers to these questions, one of the items contained in the survey of deans asked them to cite recent examples of nontraditional uses of leaves—if they were aware of any—at their college.

Approximately one-half of those surveyed cited examples that are nontraditional, at least in light of recent precedents, on their own campuses. In cases where there were none, this presumably meant that sabbaticals were limited almost entirely to activities which were directed toward teaching and scholarly work. Examples cited of nontraditional uses of leaves included: ACE fellowships in education and government, an internship in a medical clinic, service as a consultant to the Economic Development Commission of Ireland, an appointment as a research associate at the Harvard Medical School, work for the military, and work in a congressman's office. Three examples involved faculty members who were educated in one discipline and now preparing in another. These included a mathematician studying photography, an English professor studying humanistic psychology, and a German professor studying computer science. One example was of an internship in academic administration that was expected to lead to a new career opportunity.

The survey further inquired if a proposal for a leave that was not focused on research or improvement of teaching skills would be approved. Seven of the twelve deans answered yes. Of those giving a positive response, a number qualified their answer by admitting that it was more likely that a proposal would be approved for an unfunded leave which was not focused on research or improvement of teaching skills than a proposal for a sabbatical for the same purpose. One of those deans giving an affirmative response cited four examples of such leaves that had been approved at his college in the last seven years. Several noted that a significant block to using a sabbatical or even an unfunded leave for the exploration of a new career was the current requirement at most institutions that the faculty member return to the campus for at least one year following the completion of a leave of any kind.

Higher education faces a classic dilemma with regard to these less conventional uses of leave opportunities. While the need for flexibility is growing, as more and more faculty spend almost their entire careers in a single institution, so too are the pressures for restraint and conformity. Resources are more limited, and administrators feel a natural responsibility to use them as prudently and carefully as possible.

It would be foolish to suggest a dramatic expansion of the use and frequency of leaves in these days. Nonetheless, we should be careful not to unduly limit possibilities, and should try to recognize and respond to the individual needs of faculty members for special consideration at critical times in their careers. Leave policies can have an important role in that response.

## Summary

Sabbatical and unsalaried leave programs continue to serve as a principal means by which our universities and colleges provide for intellectual and professional renewal of faculty. While the traditional focus of leaves has been and continues to be on the development of the faculty member as a teacher and scholar in his or her discipline, it is also possible to take graduate courses, accept postdoctoral appointments, or do research that will lead to a broadening of or changing of academic field or even, under certain circumstances, to the exploration of a new career.

The constraints of family responsibilities and/or a spouse's career have resulted in increased difficulty in taking a leave at all, shorter leave periods, and more in-town leaves. In addition, some faculty have experienced greater difficulty in obtaining supplemental funding, which amplifies the obvious problems that result from the high costs of travel and living away from home for an extended period.

Based upon our survey, most chief academic officers would favor the practice of granting leaves not focused on research or improvement of teaching skills. Historical precedent, the prevalent requirement that faculty members return to the college for a time after the leave, and a

46

stated or implied premise that a sabbatical should benefit both the faculty member and college are factors that tend to perpetuate current practice. Specifically, the use of leaves to explore new career alternatives is not yet common.

Although the criteria for granting unsalaried leaves tend to place fewer restrictions on the activities that are possible, financial constraints generally make them a much less viable means for the exploration of alternative careers.

While the explosion of knowledge and the decline of faculty morale both plead for more frequent salaried leaves that allow for broader objectives, the economic conditions in which most of our institutions find themselves make a liberalization of current leave policies very difficult in the decade ahead.

### References

Amy, W. Private communication, October 5, 1982.
Board, W. Private communication, August 20, 1980.
Bolles, R. N. *What Color Is Your Parachute?* Berkeley, Calif.: Ten Speed Press, 1980.
Brakeman, L. Private communication, May 8, 1980.
Goldberg, H. Private communication, August 13, 1980.
Great Lakes Colleges Association. *Sabbatical Leave Policies of ACM and GLCA Colleges.* Ann Arbor, Michigan: Great Lakes Colleges Association, 1980.
Irish, J. Private communication, August 18, 1980.
Longsworth, R. Private communication, May 21, 1980.
Powell, V. Private communication, May 15, 1980.
"Sabbatical Year in University, College, and School." In P. Monroe (Ed.), *A Cyclopedia of Education.* New York: Macmillan, 1912.
Wallace, I. Private communication, November 18, 1982.
"What They're Reading on College Campuses." *Chronicle of Higher Education.* (See, for example, September 1, 1982, p. 32; September 29, 1982, p. 24; October 27, 1982, p. 20).
Wong, F. Private communication, October 4, 1982.

*David G. Marker is provost of the college and professor of physics at Hope College in Holland, Michigan.*

*Pressures mount to be more formal and legalistic*
*in evaluation procedures, but faculty evaluation*
*can still contribute to effectiveness.*

# Faculty Evaluation

*Kala M. Stroup*

## Pressures to Be Accountable, Formal, and Documented

The emphasis on the evaluation of faculty is not new, but has been given additional impetus by a number of recent changes in higher education. The trend toward accountability has focused attention on the evaluation of the performance of the faculty. Students insist upon evaluation of faculty, legislators and the public believe it should be required and more rigorous, and boards of trustees and system administrators expect systematic, thorough well-developed evaluation policies. At the same time, today's legalistic environment forces more formal, structured practices.

Parallel to these forces are the feared negative consequences of evaluation: lower morale, grade inflation, increased litigation, and a deterioration of cooperation and collegiality. These tensions within the educational community suggest a need for thorough discussion of evaluation processes and thorough analysis of the policies that guide these processes.

There are five major reasons why we should carefully develop and review our evaluation policies:

1. As it becomes more difficult to get promoted and to obtain salary increases, pressure mounts from within and without to make

J. W. Fuller (Ed.). *Issues in Faculty Personnel Policies.* New Directions for
Higher Education, no. 41. San Francisco: Jossey-Bass, March 1983.

sure our evaluations are in keeping with and do reflect merit, and are based upon established criteria. Just as it is hard to argue against the principle of differential rewards for merit in the classroom by grades, it is difficult to argue against rigorous evaluation, and therefore differing rewards.

2. It seems increasingly important to use sensitive, systematic review processes. Evaluation cannot be informal or casual. Most would prefer to rely on their own instincts and perceptions. In the academy, we are tempted to be far too intuitive and far too subjective. Many naively feel they have a sense for effectiveness and ineffectiveness, that everyone agrees with these appraisals, and that systematic reviews destroy the collegial atmosphere. Since evaluation of some type will take place, if only intuitively and unconsciously, administrators must insist that evaluations be systematic.

3. The legal environment of today allows little if any room for intuitive judgment of effectiveness. Administration of salary may well be the most litigious issue in the 1980s and 1990s. Faculty have been slowly winning concessions in the area of salary authority through persuasion, collective bargaining, and litigation. It is safe to predict that some common practices will be questioned in the next few years, for example, not giving faculty contracts along with salary figures, lack of equal pay for comparable work, merit salary increases without criteria, marketplace salary differentials without objective criteria, and evaluation without job descriptions.

4. The traditional peer-review process was once a central part of the reward system. Many believe peers are the ones sensitive and knowledgeable enough to differentiate among levels of performance and to determine the quality factors in scholarship and teaching. Yet, many forces are eroding peer-review systems, making colleagues unwilling to risk evaluating others. Some recent court decisions indicate that confidentiality will not always be protected. The goal of most institutions is to create healthy, cooperative settings, where learning can take place with a faculty who prize cooperation rather than competition. Reduced resources place the peers in the competitive mode, therefore disrupting the harmonious and cooperative environment that seems most appropriate to colleges and universities.

5. Evaluation is needed to support professional development and/or self-renewal programs. As our faculty remain on one campus for longer periods of time, professional awareness and change that result from mobility will be absent. With a stable faculty, professional development will be more important in order to maintain viability in

the academic programs. If one believes the entire lifetime should be one of learning, we must provide developmental and educational opportunities for the faculty and administration. Evaluation can help to identify those areas needing professional development.

In an era of tight resources, an increase in inquiries about accountability, and faculty impatience with administrators who do not evaluate effectively, sensitive and effective measures of evaluation are needed. Across-the-board similar treatment, regardless of performance, is not acceptable. It is important to demonstrate and document different levels of performance. At the same time, we must be sensitive to the important components of the collegial environment.

In summary, the increased pressure from outside for acountability, reduced resources, the legalistic environment, the increased need for decision making based on data, and the need for professional development programs demonstrate the mandate to review our evaluation processes and develop clear policy documents.

## Who Does the Evaluating?

Who should initiate the policy development in evaluation, determine the criteria, review each faculty member, and manage the process? Before these questions are answered, we need to believe that evaluation can be a valuable communication tool, a way of systematically forcing honest appraisal and feedback. A basic purpose of evaluation is to provide faculty members a measure of how well they are performing in their professional roles so that they can improve performance. From a realistic viewpoint, evaluation takes place whether or not it is systematic or managed. Sooner or later all evaluation activity, conscious and unconscious, serves as a basis for decision making in matters of promotion, tenure, salary increases, and other benefits. If the process is handled improperly, it can lower morale, destroy faculty incentive, reduce the momentum of the college/university, place the administrator on the receiving end of a long succession of grievances, and cost the institution time and resources.

In most institutions, the chairperson/head of the department will be the manager of the evaluation process, serving as the focal point for all information. In some smaller colleges, this will be done by the dean. The manager of the evaluation process is responsible for the evaluation procedures, the involvement of others in the process, and the assessment of benefits and costs in time and resources.

The faculty should be involved in the discussion and articulation of criteria. Shared definitions and meanings are an important part of this process. Faculty should also participate in the evaluation of colleagues, providing an assessment of quality for each of the criteria defined. The peer-review process has been a part of colleges and universities for centuries. The evaluation of the younger scholar by the senior professoriate is still central to a healthy, scholarly environment. Only the peers in the disciplines can evaluate the depth of knowledge, the significance of the scholarly works or performance, and the teaching excellence of a particular discipline.

Observing the classroom, working with colleagues in the laboratory, discussing theories, reading each other's works, evaluating the syllabus and so on can be done by peers. The internal peer-review process has been eroded by collective bargaining, legal decisions, increased federal and state monitoring, and pressures for centralization of the evaluation process. Every administrator should try to preserve as much of the peer-review process as is possible. Only peers can provide the needed qualitative judgments about discipline expertise, current information, and the vitality of a faculty member.

The details of the evaluation system must be tailored to the traditions and needs of each specific campus, but a few general principles seem important. The chairperson/head is the best manager of the process, sending forward recommendations to other levels of the institution. The chairperson/head has the key responsibility for effective policy development and systematic review in the department. The other important principle is to involve faculty in discussion of criteria and in the qualitative evaluation of others. Once major decisions are made about the management of the process, careful consideration should be given to the clear identification of the criteria.

**Definition of Criteria**

Criteria must reflect the mission of the college or university and the goals of the department. Criteria should be defined in such a way that their fulfillment gives the higher ranks dignity and stature and identifies promotions as an acknowledgment of professional accomplishment in one's discipline and leadership in one's institution. The added prestige and recognition of earned promotion and tenure based on standards of excellence contributes to the maintenance of morale and the excellence of the faculty. At the same time, the principal administrators of the institution need to make sure that the criteria for evaluation have not been so narrowly or conventionally drawn so as to discourage creativity and growth in individual careers.

*Teaching*

Teaching is a prime responsibility of the college/university. It is important to provide a standard set of procedures for evaluating teaching to assure an equitable and substantive review process. Good teaching requires continual application and effort. Teachers must keep abreast of new developments in their field and must maintain credentials as scholars, so they remain a part of the creative process by which the frontiers of knowledge are continually expanded. The teachers should be enthusiastic about their particular discipline and should be able to communicate this to their students, thus stimulating both the teacher and the students to greater achievements. Quality teaching must be a basic requirement for all faculty. Information and materials must be provided to measure the quality of teaching. The assessment should be on the level of quality, not basic performance, of the teaching function.

### Suggested Criteria for Evaluation of Teaching

1. Quality of teaching as measured by peers and student evaluations.

2. Teaching depth and breadth, that is, the number and level of courses taught.

3. Teaching load, student enrollment, number of sections taught, and number of preparations required per semester.

4. Content of courses (a review of objectives and syllabi to indicate how current and organized the courses are).

5. Additional teaching in other programs or institutions.

6. Scholarly activity encouraged among students.

7. Contributions to new course development and/or the revision of existing courses.

8. Preparation of instructional media, such as textbooks, laboratory manuals, class projects, videotape, film, slides, transparencies, individual instructional modules, and so on.

9. Experimental instructional methods and techniques.

10. Institutes, workshops, and other programs attended that are relevant to instruction.

11. Impact on students (student evaluation, pre- and post-test measures, performance on professional entry examinations, job placement, honors won, graduate school admission, and so on).

12. Graduate degree committee membership, when appropriate.

13. Theses directed, when appropriate.

*Discipline Research, Scholarly Activity, Creative Endeavor*

Scholarly and creative activities have several purposes for the faculty member. These activities maintain the competence of the teacher and provide a service to the profession and society. Accomplishments and contributions as a scholar and performer bring vital recognition to the university, to the individual, and to the learning process. The college/university exists in a large part around its ability to be continually on the forefront in the disciplines and in the knowledge of the educational process. The scholarly involvement of the faculty members demonstrates the vitality of the disciplines within the university. Promotion to assistant professor and promotion to associate professor should be based on evidence of scholarly productivity and creativity, documenting a successfully developing faculty career. For promotion to full professor, evidence must be conclusive that these objectives have been realized. Consequently, the record of scholarly and creative productivity should be substantially greater than expected at the other ranks. Continued productivity after the completion of the dissertation should be expected. As in the case of service and teaching, excellence in scholarly and creative activity alone should not be sufficient to insure promotion or merit.

*Suggested Criteria for Evaluation of Discipline Research,*
*Scholarly Activity, Creative Endeavor*

1. Publications as exemplified by papers, monographs, textbooks, and other types of scholarly publications.

2. Production, exhibition, or performances of creative work.

3. Lectures, papers, or speeches at meetings or other educational institutions.

4. Institutes, workshops, short courses, seminars, and other programs attended (related to specific areas of the discipline).

5. Research, scholarly, and/or creative endeavor grants and awards received.

6. Participation in proposal development.

7. Student research activity with graduate/undergraduate students.

8. Evidence of regional, national, or international recognition.

9. Current research, scholarly activity, and/or creative endeavor projects in progress (other than publications).

*Service*

Service is related to being a participating member of the community, the university, and/or the professional community. Professionally related extramural activities in public forums are important means of bringing prestige and recognition to the university. Service must be evaluated as to the quality of participation. In addition, the service should be in an area which contributes to the university and the fulfillment of its mission. As with teaching and research, service duties alone do not form the case for promotion or merit.

### Suggested Criteria for Evaluation of Service

1. Continuing education/public service — major continuing education programs in which the faculty member was or is participating should be mentioned, along with conferences, workshops, seminars, and so on that the faculty member sponsored.

2. University service — serving the university in teaching noncredit courses, conducting universitywide studies, serving on university committees, and serving on trustee/system committees.

3. School and departmental service — serving the school and the department by committee assignment, student counseling and advisement, and the various administrative roles such as teacher certification officer, athletic eligibility officer, assisting departmental chairperson, and so on.

4. Community service — this category would include offices held in academic, professional, and scholarly societies, public and/or governmental service/community service activities relevant to the faculty member's role at the university, and consulting activities. (Particularly for institutions located in smaller communities, service to that local community itself may also be seen as being directly in the institution's interest and appropriate for "service credit.")

### General Information

This category contains information relevant to both teaching and scholarly activity. It is mainly concerned with establishing a faculty member as a professional. Any relevant nonuniversity professional experience such as summer employment, industrial or business exchange, or sabbatical experience is appropriate. This may include professional licenses, registrations, and/or certifications; citatins in bibliographic works; awards and honors; membership in academic, professional, and scholarly societies; and other pertinent information.

## Conclusion: Criteria

These lists represent areas where it is possible to present data relevant to the evaluation decision. They should provide guidance as to sources of information to substantiate attainment and the successful fulfillment of the college/university criteria. These lists are not exclusive but they provide a framework for the criteria. Once the criteria are discussed, then the measurement and data collection become important.

## Building the Case: Methods of Data Collection

The need for models and objective methods is obvious when one examines the procedures currently in practice. There are several methods of evaluation currently in use which need to be analyzed and reviewed. Some of these may be more appropriate than others for particular institutions. In each case, the costs and benefits of the methodology are discussed.

### Activities Analysis

This procedure involves an end-of-the-year report on a standardized form describing activities and accomplishments of the year. The data generated from this procedure generally reflect some measure of quantity, but not necessarily of quality. When the Center for Research and Development in Higher Education conducted a study of university teaching for the Davis campus of the University of California (Miller, 1974, p. 10) they found that both the best and the least effective faculty members engaged in the same professional activities and allocated their time among academic pursuits in about the same way. The mere performance of activities did not assure that instruction was effective or quality was high. While an outline of activities and accomplishments is useful as a systematic way of collecting information, it is not always an indicator of the quality of performance.

### The Objective/Appraisal Method

This is a popular technique adapted from business organizations. This system does provide a framework for connecting the goals of the university/college and department with each faculty member's objectives. There are values in setting goals, defining objectives, and assessing one's movement toward these goals. These steps assist in articulating the relationship between a faculty member's performance and meeting program or departmental goals.

There are some inherent limitations. The management by objectives (MBO) method is oriented toward productivity, using the jargon of business management. The underlying assumption is that the techniques and the point of view of business planning are applicable to higher education. For example, in education goals are not always specific behavioral objectives but created opportunities. The ways in which the created climate affects others are infinite in variety. The difficulties in measuring the ability to create this atmosphere are enormous. The MBO system often misses the subtleties of creating a healthy, open environment for learning.

### Professional Growth Contract

This is an adaptation of the MBO process. Dr. Richard Gross, executive vice-president of Gordon College, reports on the use of this system (1976). The growth contract is a method of identifying the strengths and weaknesses of an individual with a plan of professional development designed to remedy these weaknesses. The process involves working through some understanding of where the individual fits most effectively within the unit. The plan for evaluation is tied to the contract. This contract has the strengths of the MBO system since it ties individual development to university needs and goals. Since the contract relates evaluation to development, it tends to be more positive and supportive of growth than other methods. It has the potential to reduce conflict between evaluation and development.

While the growth contract is certainly more in keeping with concepts considered important in higher education, its usefulness as a tool is limited. The chairperson must generate a supportive, nondefensive climate in which genuine self-assessment, evaluation, and development can take place. The inherent dilemmas in growth contracts are that the chairperson and the faculty member must share the same view of each event, that assessing growth in subject areas is often difficult, and that considerable time must be spent on resolving differing perspectives. (See related discussion under self-assessment.) Because growth contracts are designed primarily to spur personal and professional development, they are less useful for other purposes of evaluation, such as judgments about promotion and salary.

### Self-Assessment Techniques

These are important in guiding individuals to look at themselves and examine their own growth. The obvious differences in perspective and ability to be introspective among faculty members must be acknowledged. The self-assessment component is important in generating growth and change but the obvious limitations of accuracy in self-perception are very real. One's own perceptions of performance and growth are formed from an entirely different perspective, and rarely match those of others.

Research in attribution theory indicates that the observer and the actor rarely share the same world view. The actor tends to attribute causality to external factors, while the observer looks for internal causes. This differing perspective is demonstrated in research done by Jones and Nisbett (1972). The actors or the faculty members would tend to look for situational cues that elicit their behavior, whereas the observer or the evaluator would tend to focus on personality traits of the faculty.

Self-assessment becomes even more awkward when we examine other findings by attribution theorists. H. H. Kelley (1972) theorized that the attributors often act in their own self-interest, especially when attributing causality for success and failure. In an experiment on "motivated" attribution error by Johnson, Feigenbaum, and Weiby (1964), teachers conveyed arithmetical concepts to two fictitious students. Following performance feedback, attribution for the success and failure of students was ascertained. The teachers primarily attributed the poor performance in low success conditions to the students. On the other hand, when students improved significantly, the teachers ascribed the successful performance to their own teaching ability.

Beckman (1970) reports a similar finding. She included a descending performance condition in her study and examined the causal judgments of observers, as well as participating teachers. Her analysis revealed that participating teachers were more likely to attribute the ascending rather than the descending pattern of performance to themselves. On the other hand, the observers or evaluators stated that the teachers were more responsible for the high to low pattern than for the low to high.

When using self-assessment techniques, the obvious difference in perspective between evaluator and faculty member must be acknowledged. The time involved in resolution of differences must be acknowledged also.

### Role Definitions/Expectations

These are developed within the framework of the department and university and are essential for effective evaluation. They serve as a basis for the evaluation process. Negotiations take place between the faculty members and administrators in defining the role expectations. A certain core of abilities, skills, and responsibilities are developed for all faculty. In addition each position requires special skills and abilities related to the specific job assignment. Each year the administrator and the faculty member decide what needs to be strengthened or what skills need to be acquired, and then these identified skills and abilities form a growth plan. Role definitions/expectations have a semantic advantage over job descriptions by providing a clear statement of what is expected. Since most assignments must be done individually, this phase could be reflective of the administrator's expectations beyond the teaching assignment.

When such definitions are comprehensive and written, they become a useful formal record of expectations, against which evaluations of performance can be made. This is valuable when differences over evaluation lead to grievances or litigation. However, such completeness and formality may inject a bureaucratic spirit into the process, which works against goals of professional growth in a collegial atmosphere.

### Student Evaluations

These evaluations are one of the most controversial, as well as one of the most common, forms of data collection. Faculty often approach such ratings as necessary evils, with some resentment and certainly confusion about what they mean. Some of the possible negative effects come from fear and concern about the expectations for the faculty. If one believes that popularity and high rankings are the main concern of the administrator, lower morale, grade inflation, relaxation of standards, and efforts to be an entertainer in the classroom may result. Generally, student ratings of instruction are used because we want some objective data about the classroom performance and students' perception of the quality of instruction. Appropriate methods for obtaining student opinions are necessary, but such ratings should only be a part of a larger, comprehensive system of evaluation, with administrators being aware of possible negative effects of such evaluations.

When student ratings are used, careful attention should be given to the frequency, use, and types of ratings. A rating of every course, every semester, is probably too frequent. Soon the faculty gain the mistaken impression that they are teaching for a favorable rating. Since every faculty member gets conflicting information about the importance of ratings and often interprets them from a narrow point of view, the use of student ratings should be made clear. Student evaluations can provide meaningful data if appropriate acknowledgement is made of possible negative impact.

Standardized forms and the usual methods of gathering student ratings do not reflect the creativity and helpful information that might emerge if faculty were to devise different forms and methods of student evaluations. (See related discussion under rating scales.) Standardized forms tend to sacrifice distinctions and differences among disciplines for uniformity. Efforts should be made to encourage faculty to design questionnaires that yield the greatest amount of valuable information for them.

Most methods of gathering student opinions tend to yield a snapshot of satisfaction at the end of the term. Changing the time of gathering information can yield differing perspectives. Other sources of student opinions could be obtained from questionnaires given to graduating seniors, the polling of majors in a discipline, interviews with students, exit interviews for withdrawals, and the sampling of graduates.

Varying the form and the time of collection could yield additional information. Student evaluation methods must be approached with care and creativity, never losing sight of the goal of better instruction.

## Rating Scales

Such scales serve to systematize the evaluation process. The standardized form used in student evaluations of faculty is a commonly used rating scale. The strengths of the rating scale are uniformity, clarity, appearance of objectivity, and efficiency.

Rating scales have some inherent problems that limit their value. Sometimes they are not flexible enough for a wide variety of jobs. They are based on trait theory. Also, the scales give the illusion of comparability, when in actuality anchor points shift in unpredictable ways. The lack of adaptability across disciplines in faculty evaluations by students is a well-established fact. What might be valued in the teaching of chemistry is not applicable in the teaching of speech. Secondly, the assessment of personal qualities operates on the assumption that we know what traits are valuable for faculty to possess and that individuals actually possess stable personality traits. Both assumptions are open to question. In all the years that researchers have attempted to discover the traits of an effective leader, they have failed miserably. Leadership qualities are situationally specific and are not task- or content-free. The same is true of the qualities of an effective teacher.

The problem of shifting anchor points is common to most rating scales. The scale gives the appearance of comparability when in actuality the subjects often change the anchor base without being aware that they have done so. For example, "This person makes good decisions" is often rated using gender as the variable anchor, that is, "She makes good decisions for a woman." This is a different reference point from a comparison among all persons. In addition to shifting reference points, rating scales are subject to the halo effect, with the liked person high on items in the scale.

Rating scales must contain some protection against the limitation of the methodology. Scales are used because they are inexpensive and easy to administer.

*Peer Review*

This is the practice of having one's professional or intellectual colleagues evaluate the quality of one's work. This is a common practice for purpose of publication in scholarly journals, admission to external professional societies, and reviews for promotion, tenure, and merit pay. Although many are still content with the process, there are some problems of which one should be aware when developing evaluation policies.

The adequacy of the peer-review system for judging journal articles has been questioned by Ceci and Peters in a September 1982 *Change* magazine article. Using replicated articles published in top journals by authorities from prestigious institutions, they changed the name of the author and the location of the sponsoring institution. Of the ten undetected manuscripts, nine were rejected. None of the reviewers even suggested the manuscripts might be accepted for publication with rewriting. These findings are alarming, demonstrating some concern about the reliability of the peer-review process.

The other problem with local peer review is the tension created in small units. Colleagues tend to become competitive, rather than cooperative, when resources are limited. The possibility of legal action has dampened the enthusiasm for being involved in peer review. Equal opportunity laws have encouraged open procedures, which, in turn, have forced casual processes to become more formal. Faculty seem reluctant to participate.

Peer review is especially critical in the qualitative evaluation of teaching and research. Peers often can be the most helpful to other faculty in professional development by showing the way to improvement, using each other as mentors. The active involvement in evaluation of others sensitizes the faculty members to the criteria and the nuances of evaluation. This tends to clarify the process and criteria. Peer-review processes handled with care and nurturing can be very constructive.

It is sometimes useful to broaden the definition of peers. It may include not only colleagues at the same institution but also faculty in the same field teaching at other institutions. This can be particularly important at smaller institutions where faculty colleagues can be peers, evaluating an individual's contributions to the institution or influence on students, but where no one shares the same disciplinary expertise or interests. Seeking the help of peers from other institutions who do have that missing expertise can round out the peer review that takes place within small faculties.

## Conclusion: Data Collection

It should be obvious there is no clear, concise, single methodology that dominates the scene in evaluation or is, indeed, the most effective. Judicious use of a combination of tools/methods yields the most defensible assessment. Since each methodology has different costs and benefits, wise assessment of the strengths and weaknesses of each method is critical. Regardless of the method of data collection, the information is only valuable if used appropriately and within the context of the purpose for evaluation.

## Guidelines for Effective Policy Development

In developing evaluation policies for your institution, several points are important to consider.

1. The evaluation system should be embedded within the goals and mission of the department and the institution. No evaluation system can be effective without the identification of faculty roles within the context of department, school, and college or university.

2. The evaluation system should be embedded in a clear notion of what a good faculty member is, and particular attention must be given to specific areas or characteristics of teaching/service/research within the department/unit. In other words, every evaluation system must establish clear, shared definitions of the criteria within the context of the institution. Both qualitative and quantitative criteria statements are important and necessary.

3. Evaluation systems are unfair and meaningless when done without the role definition/expectation phase preceding the evaluation. Role definitions/expectations should be developed for every faculty member to the extent that they understand their relationship to others within the department, the responsibilities expected of them, and their function within the department. These definitions should be individualized according to competencies and function. Individual members of a department have different talents and expertise that contribute to

the effectiveness of the department. These differences should be maintained or enhanced in order to acknowledge diversity in departments and in the institution. On smaller campuses, different and variable assignments are necessary, making the expectation phase an even more important step.

4. Evaluations of all sorts can shape teaching. We must insure that evaluation shapes teaching in a positive manner and does not become a serious hindrance to the teaching/learning processes.

5. Evaluation must take place in an open, supportive, and positive climate. The questions about management and the utilization of the collected data need to be raised and openly discussed. Generally, the most severe critics of evaluation processes question the utilization of the data more than the importance of gathering it. Many discover too late that the decision about how the data will be utilized is as critical as the evaluation technique itself. Many failures of evaluation systems are publicly attributed to the system when, in fact, the culprit is likely to be *management* of the data.

6. The chairpersons/heads of the departments (or in small colleges, the deans) are responsible for the management of the process.

7. If professional development is an important goal and if evaluations are to be viewed as valuable feedback and useful confirmation, then the entire process must take place in a supportive, nondefensive way. This means involving faculty in the development of the criteria and of the method of data gathering.

8. Since development is so closely tied to evaluation, some self-assessment techniques should be employed. Every faculty member should be encouraged to do a self-evaluation. Each evaluation system should contain ways of addressing concerns or areas of weakness. Evaluation systems should generate genuine self-assessment, a desire to improve, and a plan for doing so.

9. Multiple sources of information are critical for fair and judicious appraisals. Obviously administrators, other faculty members, and students are part of that process. Equally important are different methods of data gathering and information gathered from a variety of sources. The array of professional activities expected are too diverse and complex to be fairly evaluated using only one source of information or one method of data gathering. Some techniques for data gathering should be process-oriented or open-ended to reflect the flexible, ongoing nature of teaching or administration. To use only static methods such as rating scales does not indicate the flexibility and adaptive nature of the work. Self-assessments, peer appraisals, student evaluations, and process-oriented methods are all necessary. These methods will give different perspectives in an attempt to gain the comprehensive

picture. When using rating scales, anchor points or comparisons must be provided.

10. No evaluation system should be too costly in money, time, or personnel. Administrators must clearly evaluate the importance of extensive evaluation systems and make every effort to weigh the time spent in such activities against the gains. Evaluation processes cannot be too costly in human relationships or resources. If developed wisely, the evaluation process can be part of the responsibilities and activities that take place routinely within the university or college.

These ten guidelines provide a philosophical stance for the review of evaluation policies. Formal evaluation is difficult and the pressures to design better systems continue to mount. These guidelines recognize that evaluation of faculty is a blend of the subjective and objective and can be viewed as part of the process of meeting the goals of the department. The responsibility for effectively managing the process belongs to the chairperson/head of the department. Clear, qualitative criteria statements and established methods of data collection are imperative for responsible, formal evaluations. The best defense is a clear policy reflective of the institution's goals and the role of the faculty in the fulfillment of those goals.

## References

Beckman, L. "Effects of Students' Performance on Teachers' and Observers' Attributions of Causality." *Journal of Educational Psychology,* 1970, *61,* 78–82.

Ceci, S. J., and Peters, D. P. "Peer Review: A Study of Reliability." *Change,* 1982, *14* (6), 44–48.

Gross, R. "Growth Contracts for Administrators." Paper presented at the 31st National Conference on Higher Education, American Association for Higher Education, Chicago, March 1976.

Johnson, T. J., Feigenbaum, R., and Weiby, M. "Some Determinants and Consequences of the Teacher's Perception of Causation." *Journal of Educational Psychology,* 1964, *55,* 237–246.

Jones, E. E., and Nisbett, R. "The Actor and the Observer: Divergent Perceptions of the Causes of Behavior." In E. Jones and others (Eds.), *Attribution: Perceiving the Cause of Behavior.* Morristown, N.J.: General Learning Press, 1972.

Kelley, H. H. "Attribution in Social Interaction." In E. Jones and others (Eds.), *Attribution: Perceiving the Cause of Behavior.* Morristown, N.J.: General Learning Press, 1972.

Miller, R. I. *Developing Programs for Faculty Evaluation.* San Francisco: Jossey-Bass, 1974.

*Kala M. Stroup is vice-president for academic affairs at Emporia State University and professor of speech communication. She serves on the executive council of Chief Academic Officers and is a commissioner for North Central Accreditation Association. She has been involved in development of personnel policies for several campuses and a statewide system.*

*A varied career presenting new challenges and opportunities*
*for development is essential to faculty vitality.*

# Variety and Productivity in Faculty Careers

*Roger G. Baldwin*

At a recent conference I was fascinated to hear a middle-aged professor
of English describe his career in higher education. For almost three
decades he had worked as a college faculty member, regularly teaching
classes, grading papers, and serving on committees. Somewhat apolo-
getically, he acknowledged that, to the casual observer, his career
might look like "dullness itself" (Hilberry, 1982).

However, closer examination revealed a rich professional life
clearly reflecting the talents and evolving interests of the professor.
What on the surface appeared to be a rather routine career was more
accurately a series of interrelated but distinct "subcareers." Over the
years he had complemented his standard teaching responsibilities with
additional professional challenges. First he served as an examiner for a
regional accrediting association. This consulting subcareer led to a
temporary position with a consortium of colleges and a major research
project studying liberal arts institutions. A second subcareer involved
administration of a humanities program jointly sponsored by twelve
colleges. A third subcareer in writing enabled this faculty member to
explore deepening interests in journalism and poetry.

The professor pursued some of his subcareers concurrently with

J. W. Fuller (Ed.). *Issues in Faculty Personnel Policies.* New Directions for
Higher Education, no. 41. San Francisco: Jossey-Bass, March 1983.

his teaching responsibilities. He worked in other subcareers during periodic leaves from teaching. Each subcareer added variety and opportunity for growth to his professional life. Each new challenge also influenced his principal role as a college teacher. Both the content and format of his teaching changed. His specialty evolved from eighteenth-century English literature to modern poetry, creative writing, and contemporary fiction. Perhaps more important than their substantive impact, however, the diverse subcareers refreshed and energized him. They maintained his enthusiasm for his ongoing role as a college English professor (Hilberry, 1982).

This brief biography is testimony to the benefits of a varied academic career. The professor profited from a supportive academic environment. Flexible policies and resources permitted his professional life to grow with changing interests and opportunities.

## The Benefits of Opportunity

Developmental research suggests that substantial change is probably fairly typical as faculty members proceed through their careers. Levinson and others' (1978) landmark study of adult development suggests that variety and diversification characterize adults' professional lives. Even if a man continues within one broadly defined occupation (such as novelist or manager), Levinson concludes, "he will go through many qualitative changes in work place, status, identity, meaning and mode of work" (p. 332). Research I conducted on professors in liberal arts colleges supports Levinson's findings. I learned that the interests, activities, problems, and goals of college teachers vary at successive career stages (Baldwin, 1979). The challenges that motivate a beginning teacher frequently differ from the ambitions of a midcareer or senior faculty member. Developmental research indicates that growth and diversification are natural and desirable attributes of the academic career. A professor's ability to continue developing, of course, depends on the availability of new responsibilities, alternative roles, and support for ongoing learning. A variety of opportunities and experiences is essential to support professional growth and vitality.

Yale sociologist Rosabeth Kanter (1977, 1978) has studied the impact of opportunity on workers' aspirations and job performance. People who perceive an opportunity to grow (the movers) in their careers develop high aspirations and become highly work involved. In contrast, people who foresee little opportunity to progress professionally (the stuck) tend to limit their aspirations, appear to become less motivated, and begin gradually to disengage from their work. Movers characteristically are energetic and highly productive. The stuck are more likely to "become passive gripers from the sidelines," what we in higher education often refer to as deadwood (1978, p. 2).

## Opportunity in the Academic Career

The strength of colleges and universities has always been a function of the quality of their faculty members. Currently, higher education institutions are even more dependent on their present human resources. Opportunities to hire new faculty have drastically diminished. In many academic departments, the core faculty today will still be the core faculty in the year 2000. Hence, in order to maintain a vigorous and up-to-date academic program, colleges must actively assist professors to continue growing personally and professionally. Their task is to preserve variety, growth opportunities, and a sense of progression in faculty careers.

Unfortunately, our definition of the successful academic career too often inhibits professors from experimenting with alternative roles and branching out into new, potentially stimulating professional areas. In *Reshaping Faculty Careers,* Todd Furniss (1981) writes that "a monolithic view of the academic career that prescribes narrowly how academics ought to see themselves inevitably forecloses options. For example, if the model dictates total devotion to a specialty throughout a life, then it also denies an acceptable place for a person who might well develop and exercise a second set of talents" (p. 63).

In many cases, higher education's devotion to specialized teaching and research locks professors into narrow career paths and forecloses many challenging vocational opportunities.

A study by the American Management Association revealed that lack of career flexibility was the largest occupational concern of middle managers. Due to their overspecialization these professionals feared that their careers were set (Schlossberg, 1977). Many academics experience a similar emotion once they have "paid their professional dues" to gain tenure and climb to the highest faculty rank. With as many as twenty to thirty years of their careers still before them, faculty in many colleges can look forward to no promotions in rank and little change in their basic responsibilities (Light, 1974).

The standard academic career, when comprised of teaching and research in a particular discipline, can demonstrate the attributes of a job with little variety and low opportunity. Promotion rates are low. There is a long timespan between moves. Principal tasks do not change substantially (Kanter, 1977).

Fortunately, a rigid career path, characterized by limited growth options, is not an inherent attribute of a college professor's life. Compared with many others, the academic career is remarkably flexible and provides a wide variety of growth options. In the role of teacher-scholar, college professors, at least theoretically, have the opportunity to take on many challenging projects and pursue new learning experiences. They can expand their personal horizons by working to master new fields of knowledge and developing new professional skills (Kanter, 1977). There are many forms of career progress in the academic profession. Advancement includes more than just elevation in rank or status.

## Who Needs Variety?

It seems reasonable to conclude that variety is an essential attribute of a successful academic career. But operationally, what do we mean by variety? What kinds of opportunities are needed to foster professors' development and vitality?

There are many ways to incorporate new experiences and ideas into a faculty member's life. Variety exists on a continuum. It may involve a slight variation in teaching duties or a radical change to research in a new disciplinary field. Changes may be temporary or permanent. To be refreshed, professors need not make a 180-degree turn in their career direction. Small variations in the academic routine (such as teaching a course with a new colleague, organizing a faculty seminar) can add the "ginger of newness" that maintains professors' interest in their responsibilities.

An individual's need for variety depends upon many variables. One's academic field, institutional type, and career stage each influence the kinds of new opportunities that can be most stimulating. Based on his analysis of the academic profession, Light concluded that "each discipline has its own history, intellectual style, distinct sense of timing, different preferences for articles and books, and different career lines" (1974, p. 12). Hence, a senior physics professor heavily involved in quantitative research may benefit from an opportunity to teach a more theoretical course on ethical issues in science and technology. In contrast, a philosophy professor might profit from released time to explore the applications of computer science to teaching logic.

In a similar way, the needs of professors vary according to the type of institution where they work. A teacher in a liberal arts college might be excited by the opportunity to collaborate with a colleague in a research institution, whereas a professor teaching specialized courses to advanced graduate students might be refreshed by an introductory course with undergraduate students.

Professors at successive career stages certainly demonstrate different problems and motivations (Baldwin, 1979). It follows, therefore, that their needs for career variety also differ. The opportunities that work for a person at one particular career stage may not work for someone at a different stage (Nelsen, 1981). For example, the traditional research sabbatical may provide exactly the right change for a young professor who wants to enhance somewhat neglected research skills. On the other hand, a midcareer faculty member may have a desire to explore the industrial applications of an academic field rather than conduct pure research. In the latter case, a short internship in a corporation might be considerably more invigorating than a standard sabbatical.

The point is that institutional policies and procedures should be sufficiently flexible to accommodate the different career needs of individual professors. If many development options are available, professors can vary their careers in the ways that will have the most beneficial impact.

### How Can Professors Vary Their Careers?

Within the framework of teaching, scholarship, and service, there are many ways to package faculty responsibilities. Faculty members and their institutions can both profit from a flexible approach to professors' duties. The objective is to create circumstances where faculty members can expand their knowledge, enhance their professional skills, and continue to feel challenged by their work. By encouraging faculty to vary their activities and interests, institutions help professors to grow in their own unique ways (Nelsen and Siegel, 1980).

*Varying Teaching Activities.* Teaching is probably the primary source of variety open to a college professor. However, because it is a professor's main responsibility, it is easy to overlook teaching as a major avenue for stimulation and growth. Faculty can vary their teaching duties by designing courses on new subject matter or by experimenting with new methods of teaching familiar material. Designing a course on a new topic can provide a teacher with a satisfying learning experience and an opportunity to be creative. Similarly, applying different teaching methods or new instructional technology provides an avenue for professional growth that is open to all professors but used too infrequently.

Teaching in a different milieu — either physical or disciplinary — can also add meaningful variety to the academic routine. Travel across departmental boundaries in the form of interdisciplinary teaching has the potential to refresh professors at the same time it expands the curriculum. Faculty exchanges to teach in other institutions perform a similar function. Professors who step out of their standard environment come in contact with different students, new colleagues, and expanded resources such as libraries and research facilities. They inevitably pick up new ideas and methods they can adapt back at their home institutions (Rodes, 1980).

An interesting variation on the faculty exchange—an intrauniversity transfer—is now in operation at the University of Kansas. Mid-career Kansas professors teach and take courses in a department or college of the University where they will develop skills and expertise different from those in their major field. The intrauniversity exchange has several advantages when compared to its interinstitutional counterpart. Professors do not need to move themselves and their families. Also, it is much easier to use newly discovered resources and maintain creative alliances when one has to travel only across campus instead of across the country to take advantage of them (Baldwin, 1981). Of course such exchanges are most feasible within fairly large institutions.

Another option is to design new teaching roles for faculty. Why should a stimulating lecturer or discussion leader share his or her talents only with students in eighteenth-century British literature classes, for example? For that matter, should not an accomplished teacher be sharing his or her expertise with interested colleagues? Novel teaching roles, if designed carefully, can provide stimulating new responsibilities at the same time they serve specific institutional needs. John Bevan, executive director of the Charleston Higher Education Corsortium, is enthusiastic about the potential impact of new teaching roles for professors. Among the roles he has suggested are:

1. *In-house visiting lecturer*—A professor proposes a broad topic or skill (such as ethics or statistics) relevant to a wide range of subject areas. The visiting lecturer may offer lectures or other learning experiences to other professors' classes, departments, or academic divisions. The visiting lecturer may also assist professors in preparing syllabi, discussion questions, visual aids, and other materials for their courses (Bevan, 1979, 1982).

2. *Faculty-conducted seminars for colleagues*—Professors use released time to prepare lectures or discussions on topics of particular interest to their fellow faculty members (Bevan, 1979).

3. *Docent in teaching*—Particularly effective professors can act as in-house consultants on teaching. A faculty docent leads seminars and workshops on teaching improvement and works individually with colleagues who want to strengthen their teaching skills (Bevan, 1982).

The range of novel faculty teaching positions is probably limited only by the creativity of professors and the constraints of academic personnel policies. By linking changing faculty interests and skills with institutional needs, custom-designed teaching positions can invigorate individual professors and their colleges.

Retraining to teach in new fields is another source of flexibility in the academic career. This option, though rarely used in the past, is gaining momentum in higher education. At twenty-two a young woman may choose to become a professor of biochemistry. But this choice does not necessarily mean that she wants to "hold forth on the same subject for nearly half a century" (Wallerstein, 1976, p. 322). It is also true that colleges do not always need the same set of skills they hired many years in the past. Fortunately, many professors' education is much broader than the area in which they now teach (Wallerstein, 1976). It is possible for some faculty to take courses or conduct independent study that will prepare them to teach in departments closely allied with their original discipline. This opportunity to vary one's career path can break the sometimes monotonous academic routine, which can be demoralizing, especially for underutilized faculty in departments experiencing declining enrollment.

*Increasing Variety Through Professional Activity.* Teaching variety may be limited by curriculum requirements or continuing student demand for certain courses. In contrast, participation in the life of one's discipline has traditionally been a flexible component of academic life. Research and scholarship activities evolve from personal interests and abilities. Hence, they offer a principal avenue for meaningful variety in the academic career. Once a professional activity no longer excites an individual, it is his or her prerogative to move on to challenging new tasks or research questions. Presenting papers at scholarly association meetings, editing journals, reviewing proposals for grant-making agencies, or consulting for government agencies each provide stimulating recognition and opportunities for continuing development. For this reason, policies that foster ongoing scholarship and other forms of professional activity can have a positive influence on professors and the institutions they serve.

Professional activity should not be confined by the boundaries of specific disciplines. Interdisciplinary studies with colleagues from other departments can stimulate career growth. Faculty can also apply their professional expertise to such critical institutional concerns as student attrition and remedial education. Scholarly activity viewed in the broadest sense can invigorate professors who long ago withdrew from the narrow and extremely competitive publications race within their own fields.

*Periods of Special Focus.* Although diversity may be a hallmark of successful academic careers, it is important to concentrate faculty efforts where they will be most effective. A rare renaissance person may be able to perform all faculty roles — teaching, research, and service — with equal zest and skill. In most cases, however, professors tend to be more adept or interested in some roles than others. Studies of faculty interests and strengths show important differences among professors at successive career stages (Baldwin, 1979; Fulton and Trow, 1974; Ladd and Lipset, 1976). For example, new college teachers generally indicate more enthusiasm for scholarly research than do their more senior colleagues.

For some professors, the opportunity to concentrate on their primary vocational interest can provide a stimulating change. If a mid-career professor of psychology has become interested primarily in teaching and mentoring students, an increased teaching load might be welcome, while also freeing departmental colleagues to spend more time on scholarly objectives that are of primary interest to them (Maher, 1981). Similarly, a professor who wishes to develop a computer course for psychology majors could devote a term or two exclusively to that project while colleagues share the regular course load. Both individual professors and their departments can benefit from differentiated staffing that permits periods of special focus on one faculty role or another. Irregular academic positions such as part-time appointments and limited-term appointments represent an effort to adapt faculty resources to changing education circumstances. Differentiated staffing patterns offer another means to meet changing program needs while varying faculty responsibilities.

*Special Faculty Projects.* The special project is another vehicle for adding variety to the academic career. Colleges and universities, like all complex organizations, encounter problems that do not fit neatly within the purview of one office or department. Ad hoc committees, special task groups, and temporary positions to address critical institutional concerns are common additions to the organizational structure of higher education institutions. These special-purpose groups or positions provide an opportunity for professors to redirect their energies and address challenging new problems. An established faculty leader may agree to spend half of his or her time chairing the college's long-range planning committee. A business professor with expertise in marketing may accept a part-time assignment consulting on a capital fund-raising campaign. A popular senior faculty member may assume responsibility for rejuvenating an institution's alumni association. Special purpose assignments of this nature provide recognition and access to new learning opportunities. As promotions do, they can motivate professors to approach their work with renewed enthusiasm.

*Temporary Nonacademic Assignments.* Occasional leaves from traditional faculty responsibilities can also stimulate professors. Variety in the academic career is frequently limited by the professoriate's definition of acceptable professional practice. Todd Furniss writes in *Reshaping Faculty Careers,* "In practice the academic community treats faculty members as if they can do acceptable work only in the subfields of their specialties. . . . It accepts the idea of trained incapacity" (Furniss, 1981, p. 79). Members of other professions, such as lawyers and engineers, travel easily across vocational boundaries. For example, it is not uncommon for a lawyer's career to move from a law firm to business to politics and perhaps finally to a judgeship. Similarly, faculty careers can benefit from movement beyond the classroom. Professors have much to offer and learn from business, government, and other employment sectors.

Faculty moves to temporary administrative positions are fairly common in higher education. The benefits of such opportunities are, for many faculty members, worth the time they must take away from their disciplinary interests. Professors face a new set of challenging problems, acquire new skills or strengthen underused abilities, and enhance their understanding of institutionwide concerns.

Temporary employment outside of the academy can also have a positive impact on faculty careers. A carefully designed internship can expose a professor to state-of-the-art knowledge, equipment, and methodology in his or her field. It can introduce a college teacher to the type of environment many students will enter upon graduation. It can also expand the circle of colleagues with whom the professor can collaborate on a wide range of professional projects (Brodsky, 1979). An internship in a federal court, for instance, can no doubt enrich the constitutional law class of an undergraduate teacher. Likewise, a one-year position at a major brokerage firm can improve a young professor's ability to counsel business students on their career options. There is little doubt that a faculty improvement leave in a nonacademic setting can provide many rich experiences a professor can draw from upon return to campus.

A flexible definition of faculty responsibilities opens almost unlimited opportunities for stimulating professional tasks. By occasionally revising their principal duties, professors can continue growing and maintain their enthusiasm for academic life. Ideally, faculty personnel policies foster this career progression.

## Supporting Career Variety:
## The Role of Academic Personnel Policy and Practice

Donald Miller (1981) defines vitality as the power to change and grow. A varied career, continually presenting new challenges and opportunities for development, is essential to faculty vitality. The academic career is multifaceted and, theoretically, offers a range of stimulating options for professors to pursue. The opportunities for variety discussed above represent only the tip of a very large iceberg. However, rigid policies, restricted resources, and lack of individualized support too often confine professors to rather routine, unimaginative careers. To maintain vigorous faculty, colleges and universities must create a climate that expects and promotes purposeful career variety.

No specific program or set of policies can guarantee rich and rewarding faculty careers. Institutions can, however, work in several critical areas to assure a climate that encourages ongoing professional growth. Academic personnel policies, resources for professional development, and supportive academic leadership can each stimulate professors to experiment regularly with exciting new professional tasks. Each area encompasses major policy issues that directly influence the worklife and performance of college professors.

*Academic Personnel Policies.* Professors build their careers on the framework provided by academic personnel policies. Evaluation criteria, guidelines for faculty leaves, and tenure and promotion policies each help to shape professors' interests and activities. In a period with limited opportunities to hire new academic personnel, policies that sustain the vitality of current faculty become especially important.

Criteria for evaluating faculty performance should reinforce professors' efforts to diversity their careers. A department chairperson will not be able to convince a young colleague to develop an interdisciplinary course if tenure guidelines only recognize teaching and research achievements in one's area of specialization. Similarly, a midcareer professor will be reluctant to negotiate a teaching exchange with a colleague from a different college if promotion criteria do not count teaching experience at other institutions. Rigid or narrow criteria of successful academic performance will directly reduce the range of challenges faculty assume. If institutions want professors to vary their teaching, research, and service activities from time to time, evaluation criteria must judge professors' contributions in relation to individual and institutional goals. A predetermined gauge of academic excellence that expects all faculty to measure up to the same standards is likely to stifle faculty initiative and promote routine careers. On the other hand, flexible evaluation criteria sensitive to individual needs for variety can foster faculty vitality.

Colleges and universities can also employ the academic reward system to encourage a wide range of constructive faculty activities. When used creatively, rewards can provide "a sense of growth, movement, progress, and value" (Kanter, 1977, p. 272). In most colleges and universities, however, the reward system is ambiguous or skewed, generally favoring the scholarship side of the academic model. What higher education institutions need are clear reward systems that encourage diversified approaches to academic careers (Nelsen and Siegel, 1980). As Everett Ladd views the situation, "we need to find better ways to encourage some faculty to emphasize quality teaching at the same time we encourage some of their colleagues at the same institution to emphasize research" (1979, p. 8).

Several types of rewards can reinforce creative faculty activity. Flexible tenure and promotion guidelines permit institutions to reward valuable faculty achievements that do not necessarily fit the mold of traditional teaching and research. Merit salary increments, where they are used, are usually reserved for significant faculty achievements in their academic field. However, they can also reward professors who have ventured into new subject areas or assumed challenging new assignments for their departments or colleges. Temporary load reduction is another means to reinforce faculty diversification. A professor who has identified a new professional interest can benefit greatly from time to expand knowledge of the field.

Less tangible rewards can also help to motivate new faculty initiatives. Dennis Showalter writes that effective institutional rewards can be as "ephemeral as the location of an office or a smile from the dean" (1978, p. 167). John Toll, president of the University of Maryland, concurs. He points out in "Rewards to Stimulate Faculty Excellence" (1980) that nonmonetary and personal rewards may become more important in the 1980s. Toll believes that "civilities that raise spirits should be encouraged" (p. 3).

Because traditional rewards (such as salary increases and promotion opportunities) are scarce in academe, some institutions have adopted new ways to reinforce continuing faculty diversification. Special awards for interdisciplinary teaching, a significant service to one's institution, or the development of skills in a new academic field can encourage innovative professional activity. An annual award providing a one-course load reduction and the responsibility to conduct a faculty seminar is one technique that may generate more research activity (Bevan, 1982). Awards targeted at specific groups can also be an effective way to use limited resources. For example, awards can be reserved for tenured professors who develop new courses or publish work in new interest areas. Used creatively, citations, small grants, or other forms of recognition can enhance the natural desire for a varied and stimulating career.

Faculty leave policies also affect professors' ability to alter their career paths. Sabbaticals have been one of higher education's principal means to revitalize faculty. However, the traditional sabbatical may be too infrequent and too research oriented to meet the diverse renewal needs of many professors in the 1980s. A wide variety of leave policies can respond to the development requirements of faculty from different fields and career stages. A sabbatical program that accepts a range of clearly defined professional growth projects (such as study in a new field or work in an industrial setting) as well as specialized research should benefit more faculty than a policy that restricts leaves to research in professors' fields of specialization. Shorter sabbaticals at more frequent intervals can help professors remain up-to-date and enthusiastic in rapidly changing fields. Internal sabbaticals, designed to utilize local resources can add variety to the careers of faculty who find it difficult to leave campus. Leave policies that facilitate movement among colleges, universities, government, and industry widen professors' exposure to new ideas and challenging professional tasks. With limited employment mobility expected during this decade, more study leaves at other universities, internships in corporations, and other short-term respites from routine responsibilities will be needed to invigorate college and university teachers. (David G. Marker reviews some of the possibilities and constraints in actual leave policies in Chapter Three.)

Flexible work-load policies are, likewise, needed to aid faculty who wish to vary their professional responsibilities. Policies requiring professors to teach a set number of courses per term leave little room for individuals to shape work around their particular interests or development needs. Similarly, policies requiring faculty to have a certain number of student advisees or committee assignments limit growth options. Work-load policies should be responsive to the objectives of individual professors and their departments. As long as everyone carries a fair share of an instructional unit's workload, it should not matter if a professor devotes more time to teaching during one term and more time to committee service during another term.

John Bevan (1982) recommends that faculty be able to bank credits for overload and independent study teaching. Under this arrangement, when a professor banks a term's worth of credit, he or she can take leave time for study or research. Adjustable work-load policies of this sort can secure time for creative aspects of the professor's role, such as writing, developing new courses, or doing research on the improvement of instruction.

*Resources for Professional Development.* Flexible policies governing work load, evaluation, and rewards can enhance the diversity and quality of professors' lives. However, additional forms of support are necessary to foster variety in faculty careers. Many of the resources needed to relieve faculty from monotonous responsibilities are already available on college campuses. Programs and policies to support faculty development have proliferated widely during the past ten years. Much of this aid helps professors to develop their specialities, in other words, to strengthen their established strengths. Parallel support is needed to help professors who wish to explore new interest areas and broaden their range of professional skills. Colleges and universities can promote variety in faculty careers by consciously aiming professional development funds and services at this objective.

Many kinds of support can assist professors who wish to place more emphasis on new or neglected dimensions of their professional lives. A college's professional development fund should be responsive to professors' needs for career variety. Hence, a funding program might award a small research grant to a senior French professor who is experiencing classroom burn-out or a retraining grant to a midcareer psychology professor who wants to teach organizational behavior in the business school. A faculty development fund that supports research and scholarship, the design of new courses, costs of professional workshops, and nonacademic internships, for example, should be sufficiently flexible to assist professors who need a meaningful break in routine.

Special-purpose faculty funds, when consciously applied, can also help professors to assume refreshing challenges. Stipends for particular kinds of projects (such as research or instructional improvement) can motivate professors to engage in growth activities they might not consider otherwise. David Marker, Provost at Hope College, reports that a program of small summer research grants upgraded scholarship and enhanced faculty morale "far out of proportion to the amount of the award" (Marker, 1980, p. 11). In the same vein, Bevan writes that minigrants for faculty stimulate professors and "seem to beget other grants" (Bevan, 1979, p. 42).

Support for professional travel is another way to alert professors to their growth options. Faculty can easily suffer from parochialism unless they interact regularly with colleagues. Attendance at disciplinary meetings and visits to other campuses are just two ways professors can gather ideas that may eventually grow into personal renewal projects.

Funds aimed at renewing specific faculty groups can likewise stimulate invigorating change. Development programs for midcareer teachers or professors in foreign languages, for example, can facilitate interesting career adjustments right where they may be needed most. A dean's discretionary fund can serve much the same purpose. It enables the dean to catalyze specific career adjustments with "carefully aimed monetary support" (Nelsen, 1981, p. 25).

Institutions can also foster professors' development by establishing new outlets for creative work. On-campus vehicles for professional activity, such as a faculty lecture series, research symposia, or an in-house research journal, can enhance the scholarly climate at a college or university while they add another dimension to the careers of college teachers (Bevan, 1982). A faculty internship program in industry or a rotating professorship in interdisciplinary studies are added examples of the initiatives colleges can take to add more variety to faculty careers.

Support for professional development is a powerful change agent. It permits faculty to pursue their natural inclination to learn and grow. Professional development policies that recognize the value of varied faculty careers can contribute to the overall quality of professors' work life.

## The Role of Academic Leadership

Academic personnel managers such as department chairpersons and deans have particularly vital roles to play in the support system that sustains variety in faculty careers. They can stimulate professional growth by setting high achievement standards. They can support a campus climate where varied career activities are expected and reinforced. Nelsen writes that the department chair's "most important responsibility should be the recruitment, evaluation, development, and continuing renewal of department faculty" (Nelsen, 1981, p. 55). Deans have much the same responsibility at a broader level. Policies and programs established to encourage career diversity must have strong administrative backing before they will influence professors' behavior. When deans and department chairpersons hold faculty accountable for their professional renewal efforts, professors are likely to take this responsibility seriously.

However, academic leaders' role in the renewal process is principally catalytic rather than judgmental. One major task is to help professors identify their professional problems and growth needs. It is sometimes difficult for college teachers, as for all adults, to be open and honest about their need for self-renewal (Nelsen, 1981). Deans and department chairs have many opportunities to stimulate useful career examination. Providing feedback on formal evaluations, inquiring about research interests, and asking about future career plans can all start professors thinking about steps to advance their career development.

Academic leaders have a responsibility to keep faculty informed about their renewal options in teaching, scholarship, and other professional activities. Professors are often unaware of the diverse opportunities available to them. Nelsen (1980) concludes that administrative leadership is particularly important in development areas where faculty are reluctant to take the initiative. A professor may only consider designing an interdisciplinary course or spending a term in the university's budget office if the suggestion comes from a respected academic leader.

Administrative support is very important as professors weigh their development options and assume new career challenges. Deans and department chairpersons have critical roles to play in matching professors with the kinds of tasks that will most effectively stimulate their development (Miller, 1981).

Persons in academic leadership positions can use the resources at their discretion to encourage professors to alter their career paths. As discussed previously, small grants or released time, when targeted carefully, can introduce faculty to important growth opportunities. Deans and department heads can reinforce professors' growth by rewarding those who take on challenging new assignments or develop competence in additional academic fields. Essentially, academic leaders can maintain a stimulating academic work environment by careful manipulation of institutional policies and resources.

## Conclusion

Colleges and universities should assess the impact of their personnel policies and practices on faculty careers. Does the institutional environment encourage professors to experiment with challenging new tasks? Does it help them to expand their range of skills? Or do institutional values confine professors to routine assignments and limited growth opportunities? Faculty resources are too precious to waste. A rigid personnel system that fails to respond to individual talents and growth needs is costly to professors and the institutions they serve.

A college's values are evident in the components of its faculty personnel system. A higher education institution that appreciates the benefits of varied faculty careers will develop incentives for career flexibility. Evaluation criteria and promotion and tenure guidelines will consider professors' efforts to diversify their professional lives. Support for professional development will be available for faculty members who want to branch out in new career directions. Work assignments will reinforce professors' growth efforts. If colleges and universities encourage professors to adapt their careers to emerging interests and opportunities, they will be exciting places — places where English teachers and other professors remain engaged in their work.

## References

Baldwin, R. G. "The Faculty Career Process — Continuity and Change: A Study of College Professors at Five Stages of the Academic Career." Unpublished doctoral dissertation, University of Michigan, 1979.

Baldwin, R. G. "Planning and Action on Campus." In R. G. Baldwin and others (Eds.), *Expanding Faculty Options.* Washington, D.C.: American Association for Higher Education, 1981.

Bevan, J. M. "Faculty Evaluation and Institutional Rewards." *Improving Undergraduate Education in the South.* Atlanta: Southern Regional Education Board, 1979.

Bevan, J. M. "The Chairman: Product of Socialization or Training?" In G. French-Lazovik (Ed.), *Practical Approaches to Evaluating Faculty Performance,* New Directions for Teaching and Learning, no. 11. San Francisco: Jossey-Bass, 1982.

Brodsky, R. F. "A New Type of Faculty Improvement Leave." *Engineering Education,* 1979, *70* (3), 271-276.

Fulton, O., and Trow, M. "Research Activity in American Higher Education." *Sociology of Education,* 1974, *47* (1), 29-73.

Furniss, W. T. *Reshaping Faculty Careers.* Washington, D.C.: American Council on Education, 1981.

Hilberry, C. "Reflections on the Nature of a Teaching Career." *GLCA Faculty Newsletter,* March 12, 1982, pp. 3-4.

Kanter, R. M. *Men and Women of the Corporation.* New York: Basic Books, 1977.

Kanter, R. M. "The Changing Shape of Work: Psychosocial Trends in America." In *Current Issues in Higher Education.* Washington, D.C.: American Association for Higher Education, 1978.

Ladd, E. C., Jr. "The Work Experience of American College Professors: Some Data and an Argument." Paper presented at the 1979 National Conference on Higher Education, Washington, D.C., April 1979.

Ladd, E. C., Jr., and Lipset, S. M. "The Aging Professoriate." *Chronicle of Higher Education,* May 26, 1976, p. 16.

Levinson, D. J., and others. *The Seasons of a Man's Life.* New York: Knopf, 1978.

Light, D., Jr. "Introduction: The Structure of the Academic Professions." *Sociology of Education,* 1974, *47* (1), 2-28.

Maher, T. "Designing New Roles within Academe." In R. Baldwin and others (Eds.), *Expanding Faculty Options.* Washington, D.C.: American Association for Higher Education, 1981.

Marker, D. G. "Improving the Scholarly Climate on Campus Through a Program of Small Grants." In W. C. Nelsen and M. E. Siegel (Eds.), *Effective Approaches to Faculty Development.* Washington, D.C.: Association of American Colleges, 1980.

Miller, D. B. "Training Managers to Stimulate Employee Development." *Training and Development Journal,* 1981, *35* (2), 47–50, 52–53.

Nelsen, W. C. "Faculty Development: Perceived Needs for the 1980s." In W. C. Nelsen and M. E. Siegel (Eds.), *Effective Approaches to Faculty Development.* Washington, D.C.: Association of American Colleges, 1980.

Nelsen, W. C. *Renewal of the Teacher-Scholar: Faculty Development in the Liberal Arts College.* Washington, D.C.: Association of American Colleges, 1981.

Nelsen, W. C., and Siegel, M. E. "Faculty Development: Promises, Realities, and Needs." In W. C. Nelsen and M. E. Siegel (Eds.), *Effective Approaches to Faculty Development.* Washington, D.C.: Association of American Colleges, 1980.

Rodes, J. "Faculty Exchange: Overcoming Academic Calcification." In W. C. Nelsen and M. E. Siegel (Eds.), *Effective Approaches to Faculty Development.* Washington, D.C.: Association of American Colleges, 1980.

Schlossberg, N. K. "Breaking Out of the Box: Organizational Options for Adults." *Vocational Guidance Quarterly,* 1977, *25* (4), 313–318.

Showalter, D. E. "Publication and Stagnation in the Liberal Arts College." *Educational Record,* 1978, *59* (2), 166–172.

Toll, J. S. "Rewards to Stimulate Faculty Excellence." *National Forum,* 1980, *62* (2), 3–4.

Wallerstein, G. "Faculty Changing Departments: Why, Who, and When?" *AAUP Bulletin,* 1976, *62,* 322–324.

*Roger G. Baldwin is assistant to the provost at Wittenberg University. From 1980–82 he was a research associate at the American Association for Higher Education. While at AAHE, he conducted a nationwide study of college and university programs designed to expand professors' career options.*

*A role for retirement plans in effecting personnel change*
*is suggested by low turnover of tenured faculty and*
*higher mandatory retirement ages. Early- or phased-retirement*
*options can be offered.*

# Faculty Retirement: Early, Normal, and Late

*Francis P. King*

The objective of a faculty retirement plan is to provide a reasonable replacement of salary when paid work ceases and retirement begins. In addition, a pension plan incorporates other personnel policy goals. Properly structured, it aids in recruitment and retention of faculty. It should also facilitate preretirement separation, permitting faculty mobility among institutions without loss of pension benefits (AAC-AAUP, 1980, p. 321).

As an economic and social instrument, a faculty retirement plan must be responsive to changing conditions, including relevant legislative changes. To assure maximum utility, its near-term effectiveness should be periodically reviewed. Its success in achieving long-term goals must also be monitored.

Declining enrollments and low faculty turnover raise the question of how an institution's retirement provisions might aid in responding to current personnel problems. This chapter addresses six major elements appropriate for retirement policy review: (1) normal-age benefits and goals, (2) mandatory retirement, (3) early retirement, (4) phased retirement, (5) auxiliary retirement savings programs, and (6) retirement counseling.

J. W. Fuller (Ed.). *Issues in Faculty Personnel Policies.* New Directions for
Higher Education, no. 41. San Francisco: Jossey-Bass, March 1983.

## Normal-Age Benefits and Goals

The age designated for normal retirement by a pension plan is generally the age at which the plan's benefit level becomes sufficient to make retirement economically feasible. The combination of the normal age and its benefit level is an expression of the plan's goal. Retirement benefits at earlier ages fall short of the goal because of applicable actuarial reductions. The joint AAC — AAUP "Statement of Principles on Academic Retirement and Insurance Plans" (1980) notes that "the stated normal retirement age may be earlier than or may coincide with the mandatory retirement age" (p. 322). It adds that "plans in which the normal retirement age is set within the age range of sixty-five to seventy appear to conform with reasonable practice."

The normal-age benefit level will influence the cost and practicability of early retirement supplements and phased retirement arrangements. Therefore, in examining a retirement plan for its potential in advancing various personnel objectives, analysis should start with scrutiny of a plan's current normal-age benefit objective and with the plan elements that determine whether individuals reaching the normal age will receive the benefits that the plan intends them to have.

Pension benefit objectives are generally stated as replacement ratios, that is, retirement benefit as percent of final earnings. The benefit ratio recommendation of the AAC-AAUP joint statement (1980) for normal-age retirement for persons who have participated in a plan for at least thirty-five years, combining the pension and social security, is "an after-tax income equivalent in purchasing power to approximately two-thirds of the yearly disposable salary (after taxes and other mandatory deductions) during the last few years of full-time employment" (pp. 322–323).

The after-tax or disposable income replacement concept adopted by the joint statement provides a practical meausurement of a retirement plan's results. While after-tax income may vary somewhat among persons with the same gross income, the disposable income idea contributes to a more realistic assessment of individual economic well-being than does the before-tax ratio. This is because total deductions from salary in working years (for income taxes, Social Security taxes, and benefit plan contributions) are generally much higher as a proportion of total gross income than are comparable deductions during retirement years. In retirement, Social Security benefits are not taxed as income, double exemptions are granted people over age sixty-five, and retirees are usually in lower tax brackets. There are no more Social Security taxes or pension plan contributions. Hence, disposable income in retirement is likely to be a higher percentage of gross income than before retirement.

Retirees are sometimes unaware of just how much higher the after-tax ratios are. For example, for a professional-level employee retiring at age sixty-five after thirty-five years of service, a pension benefit (expressed as a single life annuity) from a 10 percent defined contribution plan might provide about 35 percent of final years' earnings, or about 1 percent for each year of service (TIAA-CREF, 1978, p. 7). The Social Security benefit (the Primary Insurance Amount) might represent another 25 percent of final earnings, assuming a taxable wage history at or near the upper end of Social Security's taxable wage base. Combining these benefits produces a before-tax replacement ratio of about 60 percent of final earnings. The benefits after taxes, in contrast, can amount to as much as 85 percent of the preretirement *disposable* income. Because of the weighting of Social Security benefits in favor of lower-income people, this after-tax ratio would be even higher for people at the lower end of the pay scale, but lower for those at the high end.

In addition to a pension plan's contribution rate, many factors will influence the dollar amount of a plan participant's benefits: rates of investment return, rates of salary increase over periods of plan participation, mortality rates, vesting provisions, and, importantly, gaps in plan participation. For more precise indications of benefit levels under a specific plan, administrators may want to request benefit projections for current plan participants. These will denote the plan's current effectiveness in meeting normal-age benefit goals that may have been established many years ago.

In looking at benefit projections of actual plan participants — perhaps for faculty aged fifty-five and over, to start with — administrators may be in for some surprises. Such projections often reveal plan weaknesses that ought to have been corrected but have not been. Frequently, the cause of lower-than-expected benefits lies in a plan's provisions for participation, which may be voluntary rather than required. Employees who currently participate in a voluntary plan may nevertheless have substantial coverage gaps because they delayed enrolling in the plan. It may be hard to understand the thinking of employees who fail to participate in a contributory plan (one that requires an employee contribution), thereby giving up substantial employer contributions to their future well-being. But such actions are not infrequent in the history of voluntary pension plans and are the reasons most pension plans require participation at some point.

The AAC-AAUP statement of principles recommends that plan

participation be required "after not more than one year of service by all full-time faculty and administrators who have attained a specified age, not later than thirty" (AAC-AAUP, 1980, p. 322). Where this participation standard is not met, appropriate plan amendments can strengthen the plan over the longer term and help make life easier for administrators in future decades. It may take some years, though, for benefit projections of participants to reflect improved benefit levels resulting from longer participation.

Specific benefit projections can identify the individuals who will arrive at early or normal retirement ages with low pension benefits due to periods of nonparticipation in a voluntary plan, or for other reasons. They will be in a poor position to take advantage of special early-retirement supplements or even to retire at the normal age, and are likely to be prominent among those who stay on beyond the normal age.

Many faculty reaching retirement age after a career of job mobility have moved among institutions with continued retirement coverage under the immediately vested and portable annuity contracts issued by TIAA-CREF. Their retirement credits will include the benefits acquired through those plans and the result may be likened to career participation in a single plan (Furniss, 1981, p. 140).

On the other hand, some faculty will have joined the plan in midcareer, coming from plans with delayed vesting. Ten years of service is a frequent vesting requirement in business and industrial plans and public employee retirement systems (Bankers Trust Co., 1980, pp. 14–17; Cook, 1981b, pp. 7–8). Service terminated short of the required vesting periods will not have earned pension accruals or accumulations in these prior plans. These employees may exhibit a lower propensity to retire before their last employer's mandatory retirement age.

Another possible cause of low benefits at retirement results from provisions that permit employee cash withdrawals from the pension plan during working years or at retirement (McGill, 1975, pp. 124–125). The AAC-AAUP statement of principles (AAC-AAUP, 1980, p. 323) recommends that payment of accumulated pension funds be only in the form of a life annuity, with possible exceptions for cashouts at retirement of small portions of an accumulation, or of small accumulations in inactive accounts. A plan that permits cash withdrawals defeats its purpose of assuring a monthly retirement income for life, including a survivor income benefit, if elected.

In summary, a plan review, including analysis of benefit projections of current participants, can (1) help uncover plan weaknesses and map the development of appropriate amendments, and (2) help build up the kind of information needed to develop strategies for post–normal-age retirement, early retirement, and phased retirement.

## Mandatory Retirement

When the age for earliest mandatory retirement was raised from sixty-five to seventy by the 1978 amendments to the Age Discrimination in Employment Act of 1967 (ADEA), the labor department ruled (*Federal Register,* 1979) that the ADEA amendments did not change pension regulations under the Employee Retirement Income Security Act (ERISA) and that pension plans were not required to continue benefit accruals or defined contributions past age sixty-five. The labor regulations were later affirmed by the Equal Employment Opportunity Commission, which assumed jurisdiction over age discrimination legislation in 1979 (*Federal Register,* 1981).

Nevertheless, the majority of retirement plans covering faculty in higher education continue retirement benefit credits for service after the normal age. Among TIAA-CREF plans in colleges and universities using normal retirement ages below seventy, 76 percent continue plan contributions after the normal retirement age (Cook, 1981a, p. 310). Public employee and state teacher systems covering faculty generally continue formula benefit accruals to the date of retirement, although some plans limit the service factor in the formula to a maximum number of years, ranging from thirty to forty years (Cook, 1981b, pp. 5–7).

Might continued accruals and contributions operate to delay faculty retirement beyond the normal age? Probably not, if pension benefits plus Social Security starting at age 65 are adequate. Probably so, if for one reason or another retirement at age sixty-five is not financially feasible. A study of TIAA-CREF retirement plan participants aged sixty years and over (Mulanaphy, 1981, p. 23) found that participants rated assurance of an adequate retirement income the most important of seventeen listed factors in the retirement decision. There is little other research evidence in this area, partly because the 1978 ADEA amendments have been in effect a relatively short time, and partly because research design would require the management of many variables and present difficult problems in selecting representative study populations. Perhaps the best that can be done currently by college administrators who aim for a high rate of normal-age retirements is to make sure that retirement benefits are at reasonable levels at normal ages, that retirement counseling is provided, and that the tax-deferred programs for extra retirement savings for educational employees are available to employees on the campus and that their advantages are well understood.

## Early Retirement

Pressures of declining student enrollments, budgetary constraints, decreased federal programs, and changes in educational objectives have suggested early retirements as a means of rather quickly achieving desirable changes in faculty profile. Further thoughts about the potential of early retirements resulted from the increase to age seventy of the earliest age for mandatory retirement (the 1978 ADEA amendments) and by the expiration in mid-1982 of a temporary exception for tenured employees to the age-seventy retirement rule.

An early retirement under a private pension plan is usually understood to mean one that takes place prior to the stated normal retirement age. Since the normal age in most college and university pension plans is sixty-five (King and Cook, 1980, pp. 105–109; TIAA-CREF, 1982d, pp. vi, viii), early retirement is usually regarded as retirement before age sixty-five. Public retirement systems may have two or more normal retirement ages; for example, a normal age of sixty-five may be accompanied by a lower normal age for participants who have met a service requirement (Cook, 1981b, pp. 10–11).

Can retirement after sixty-five be "early"? The increase to seventy as the first age at which retirements can be mandated has suggested to some observers (Edwards, 1982, p. 11) that retirement at any age before seventy might be considered early and that normal-age retirement at sixty-five is, in fact, an early retirement. The broadened age range for voluntary retirements now spans at the very least a ten-year period from ages sixty to seventy.

It is probably too early to discern whether or to what extent the new age discrimination rules will cause retirements to shift upward from the normal age. In 1980, the majority of TIAA-CREF annuities were begun at age sixty-five or under (TIAA-CREF, 1981, p. 2). Assuming that pension-benefit levels will be adequate for normal-age retirement and above, the challenge for early retirement incentive programs lies in stimulating retirement prior to the normal age by offering financial inducements.

Congress may further extend the range of retirement choice by uncapping the top age. In the 1980–81 academic year, 95.8 percent of full-time faculty members with the rank of professor had tenure (National Center for Education Statistics, 1981, p. 5). Even if an exception is provided that will continue mandatory age-seventy retirement for tenured employees, postsecondary institutions may expect to have a high proportion of tenured faculty for some time to come (Consortium on Financing Higher Education, 1980, p. 5; U.S. Congress, House Select Committee on Aging, 1981, p. 253). In this light, the operating question is how the retirement program might help make room for entry-level faculty and open up the tenure track.

With early retirement defined as retirement before an institution's stated normal retirement age, the extent to which an early retirement incentive program can help achieve desired personnel goals will depend on the age structure of faculties and the financial resources available. If relatively few faculty fall within the age group for which early retirement is practicable, there is little point in exploring further. If the personnel profile suggests the appropriateness of an early retirement program, the next questions are: (1) What are the available financial resources? and (2) How can they be matched to the income needs of potential candidates for early retirement?

From a financial standpoint, retirement before the normal age is likely to be most feasible for employees with long service who have been accumulating annuity contributions or credited service accruals over a full career. For those whose academic careers have included a number of job changes, feasibility will be related to the pension vesting and portability achieved under the plans of prior employers, either in business and industry or in the educational field. Here, the variables of employment history and vesting of plan benefits may determine whether early retirement can be made attractive.

Incentives for early retirement may be offered on a selective individual basis or may be stated in formal terms with announced provisions for an eligible group (Jenny, Heim, and Hughes, 1979, pp. 34–44). A time limit may be set on the incentive program's availability. The purpose of a limited "window" for early retirement is to stimulate thinking, planning, and decision making about early retirement, as well as to help make it financially possible. Too narrow an aperture may be criticized, however, as encouraging individuals to plunge too quickly into an unplanned retirement.

Voluntary early retirement incentive programs that open a window of opportunity differ from the statutory early-retirement provisions frequently found in state employee and state teacher retirement systems. Early retirement provisions in public plans provide for actuarially reduced benefits beginning at stated ages or function primarily as rewards for long-service employees by incorporating age and service requirements that automatically qualify employees for actuarially unreduced formula benefits at ages under sixty-five.

Employee eligibility for early-retirement incentive programs may be defined in terms of age, employee classification, salary classification, service, or any combination of these (Jenny, 1974, pp. 3–4). After developing a tentative formula for eligibility, the institution will want to look at the projected retirement benefits of the eligible group for both normal-age retirement and early retirement. This will enable comparisons of incentive benefits with those that would normally accrue to employees were they to continue in service rather than retire. There should also be an analysis of salary amounts that will be forgone in the event of early retirement, a question of some interest to both employee and employer. These determinations will help in setting appropriate levels of early-retirement benefits and will permit estimates of the potential costs of the plan. The estimates may suggest redefinitions of eligibility that will help increase or decrease the number of potential takers.

An incentive plan for early retirement should not ignore the role of Social Security. If eligibles are to include faculty under age sixty-two (the earliest retirement age under Social Security), the plan may want to take into account the absence of a Social Security income component until that age, as well as the lower Social Security benefits payable upon retirement at age sixty-two than upon retirement at age sixty-five. An employee's Social Security benefit is reduced by 5/9 of 1 percent for each month that retirement takes place before age 65, a 20 percent reduction for retirement at age sixty-two. If the countable years of Social Security coverage are reduced because employment ceases prior to age sixty-two, there may also be reductions in Social Security benefits based on the "average indexed monthly earnings" used in the calculation of benefits (Social Security Administration, 1982, pp. 100, 109–110).

For administrative convenience and for clarity of communications with eligible staff members, the benefit stream under the early retirement program may be identified as two successive elements: income benefits from the date of early retirement to normal age sixty-five and benefits after age sixty-five. For example, a bridging amount of monthly income may be paid directly by the institution to the retiree from the date of early retirement at or before age sixty-two to age sixty-five; the Social Security benefits (although reduced) might also be started at age sixty-two. Concurrently, the institution would pay an amount into the individual's TIAA-CREF annuity that would be sufficient to provide that the TIAA-CREF annuity when started at age sixty-five (the termination age for the bridging benefit) would be at the same level that it would have been had the individual continued in employment until age sixty-five under stated salary assumptions. After age sixty-five, benefits would consist solely of annuity income and Social Security.

Another approach is simply to provide for the start of the regular retirement annuity on the date of early retirement (rather than at age sixty-five) at a benefit level at or close to the level of benefits for retirement at age sixty-five. This would require a single additional annuity premium, the amount of which would be determined by the additional benefit to be purchased and the longer life expectancy over which income benefits would be expected to be received.

An institution may expect to examine and test a number of different patterns and amounts of early retirement incentive benefits before it selects one that seems best to meet its needs. If benefits are to be provided by additional premium payments to individually owned annuity contracts, it will be necessary to observe the limitations of such contributions under sections 415 and 403(b) of the Internal Revenue Code (Heller, 1979, pp. 10–23). Contributions to college-owned annuity contracts rather than to the individually owned annuity contracts used under the institution's retirement plan may be appropriate in some situations. An early retirement plan should comply with the requirements of ERISA and ADEA. The plan should be fully reviewed by counsel before adoption.

An institution's expenditure for an incentive early-retirement plan will be a function of the cost of the additional benefits less the projected compensation expense of continued employment. The overall value may be measured in terms of net financial expenditures plus the other personnel objectives underlying an incentive plan—the freeing up of tenured positions, opportunities to recruit and develop younger faculty, and achievement of other institutional objectives.

An incentive early-retirement plan will not be complete if its relation to participation in other employee benefit plans is not spelled out. Except for disabled persons, eligibility for Medicare coverage does not start until age sixty-five, so health coverage will be of particular concern to persons considering early retirement. Provision for continuation of health plan coverage as part of the employer's group will enhance the attractiveness of a plan and will contribute to its acceptability. Many employers provide continuation of health plan coverage for retirees (King and Cook, 1980, pp. 192–193), with wraparound or major medical benefits supplementing Medicare for retirees and their spouses after they reach age sixty-five.

A retirement incentive plan may also be useful as a means of encouraging retirements after reaching the stated normal age. Employees who might otherwise continue in service after age sixty-five might be tempted to retire through a time-limited severance-pay offer, for example. Two years of salary in form of severance pay could be provided to employees who accept voluntary retirement at age sixty-five, one year at age sixty-six, one-half year at age sixty-seven, with the offer terminating after age sixty-seven. It is hard to determine, however, whether offers of this type tend to attract those who would retire at these ages anyway.

Unless the early-retirement incentive program is an attractive alternative to continued employment, response to it may be disappointing. A carefully developed communications program should be instituted as a means of avoiding misunderstanding or misinterpretation of the program or its purpose. Retirement counseling programs can aid personal preparation for retirement and help make the transition easier.

## Phased Retirement

In some circumstances and for some faculty, phased retirement may be an attractive option. Over a stated period, phased retirement provides for reduced work load and salary, leading to full retirement. Phased retirement is usually worked out on an individual basis, tailored to each situation, but it may be offered generally to eligible faculty on a uniform basis. Furniss (1981, pp. 121–125) describes the details of generally offered programs in a private university and in two state university systems.

Phased retirement is a suitable option for faculty members who wish to continue working until normal retirement but would prefer reductions of teaching or research responsibilities from current levels. For the institution, phased retirement may accord well with planned changes in course offerings and changes in departmental enrollments. The flexibility of possible arrangements helps make phased retirement closely responsive to individual and institutional goals.

When reductions in work loads are arranged, corresponding reductions in salary may not be in the same proportion. A one-third reduction in work load may be accompanied by a one-fourth reduction in salary. This kind of relationship may make phased retirement more attractive. Or, reductions in work and pay may be on a one-to-one basis, to many a fair and attractive relationship. A written agreement is the best way to cover the various aspects of phased retirement with progressive reductions in work load and salary. For a three-year phasing period beginning at age sixty-two, for example, the first year's reduction might be specified as one-third, with a salary reduction of one-fourth. The next year the work load would be reduced to one-half, the pay to two-thirds. In the final year before retirement, the work load would drop to one-third, with salary reduced to one-half.

With contributions to the retirement plan stated as a percentage of salary, it is evident that pension contributions on behalf of faculty who elect phased retirement will be lower than if full salary continued to age sixty-five. With lower contributions, benefits at retirement will be lower. Therefore, when the goal of phasing out includes making retirement more attractive at the end of the specified phasing period, it may be desirable to provide an income amount at retirement that is about the same as if the phased reductions had not been made. This may be done by increasing the contribution rate as a percentage of salary or by making specified extra contributions during the phasing period.

The proportion of salary represented by the employer's annuity contributions must fall within the employee's exclusion allowance under sections 415 and 403(b) of the Internal Revenue Code. If, because of the reduced salaries during phasing periods, the remaining exclusion allowance is insufficient to permit the necessary employer contributions, they may be made to a separately maintained, employer-owned annuity contract.

Interested faculty members should be made aware of the effect of phased retirement on Social Security benefits. When salary is reduced below the amount of the taxable wage base, future Social Security benefits may be lower, although in most cases the reduction would not be expected to be substantial.

## Extra Retirement Savings Programs

For many retired faculty, income based on prior savings and investment contributes substantially to total income (Mulanaphy, 1974, p. 21). With Social Security and pension benefits as a base, additional income from savings can help transform retirement from ordinary to enjoyable. The savings process is an important part of preparing for retirement, and employer assistance can help advance it for faculty and staff.

*Tax-Deferred Annuities.* Employees of educational institutions are in an especially favorable position to save for retirement through the use of tax-deferred annuities (TDAs) under section 403(b) of the Internal Revenue Code. TDAs permit the investment of savings before federal income tax (and, often, state tax) through "salary reduction," and also allow for the accumulation of investment earnings without being currently taxable as income. Taxation is deferred until income is received during retirement, when the individual may be expected to be in a lower tax bracket.

The primary leverage in TDAs is in the availability of the larger before-tax amount for investment and in the deferral of taxes on the compounding investment earnings, whatever the tax bracket in retirement (Bernstein, 1981, p. 190; Employee Benefit Research Institute, 1981, p. 4). Over a twenty-year savings period, for example, in a 30 percent marginal tax bracket, the accumulation from a $100-per-month, TDA salary-reduction amount earning 12 percent interest would be $120,808. The alternative $70 per month of after-tax investments with earnings taxed each year would accumulate to $60,056. In higher tax brackets the difference is greater. (These figures allow for a 1.5 percent front-end investment expense charge.)

Before-tax TDA savings programs require the cooperation of educational employers. A salary reduction agreement between employer and employee must be signed. This provides that the employer will pay a portion of the employee's salary to the TDA each month and that the balance will be the salary amount reported for federal income tax purposes.

The maximum contribution that may be paid through salary reduction to a TDA each year is subject to specified limits. Generally, the amount available for extra savings depends on the amount of the employer's contributions to the regular defined contribution retirement plan or on a special formula under a defined benefit plan. If the employer's defined contribution to the regular retirement plan is 5 percent, salary reduction for the extra TDA may be as much as 12.5 percent; if the employer contributes 10 percent, the remaining permissible reduction would be about 8 percent (TIAA-CREF, 1982c, p. 5). Certain available "special elections" appropriate for some individuals provide for larger salary reduction amounts.

If salary reduction amounts used to purchase TDAs reduce salary below the maximum amount of the taxable wage base for Social Security, the reduction amounts are still counted as wages for Social Security purposes.

*Qualified Voluntary Employee Contributions.* An additional tax-deferred savings opportunity — Qualified Voluntary Employee Contributions (QVECs) — was introduced by the Economic Recovery Tax Act of 1981. QVECs are similar to the Individual Retirement Accounts (IRAs) that may be purchased by individuals on their own from banks, mutual funds, and insurance companies, except that QVECs take the alternative form of voluntary employee contributions to a qualified employer plan (regular or supplementary) that may be deducted from the employee's gross income for federal income tax purposes. QVEC deductions are not permitted after an employee reaches the age of seventy years and six months. As with TDAs, interest and investment earnings on QVECs are not taxed as income until later, when benefits are received. Unlike TDAs, however, any benefits or cash withdrawals taken before the age of fifty-nine years and six months are subject to an additional 10 percent income tax penalty (except for death or disability).

Contributions under a QVEC plan may generally be made up to a maximum limit of $2,000 per year. A QVEC is an alternative to an IRA, so that if a maximum contribution is made to a QVEC, no additional contributions may be made to an IRA, except that if an employee has a nonworking spouse, an additional $250 contribution to a separate spousal IRA may be made (TIAA-CREF, 1982b, p. 4).

*TDAs and QVECs Together.* The potential for added employee savings for retirement on an advantageous tax-deferred basis, already substantial through the use of TDA contributions, is further enhanced by the newer QVECs and IRAs. The employer plays a central role in the administration of TDAs and QVECs by establishing the plans and preparing the agreements for salary reduction (TDAs) and employee contributions (QVECs). Employees whose family responsibilities may be lessening may find these special tax-favored instruments very helpful in improving financial prospects in retirement. The employer is in a strong position to provide information about the advantageous savings possibilities of TDAs and QVECs for faculty and staff, and to encourage their use.

## Retirement Counseling

The transition from work to retirement can represent a profound change in life patterns. For some, just the thought of retirement is disturbing; retirement planning may be ignored or delayed until the last minute. With the new higher age of mandatory retirement (and its possible elimination), opportunities for delay are increased. Timely retirement will be more likely if it is based on sound preparation for retirement, as will the likelihood of retirement being a satisfactory and rewarding time of life.

In this situation, retirement counseling and planning assistance emerge as important issues of employer–personnel policy. If the retirement decision is to be given the careful and thoughtful consideration it deserves, it cannot be a last-minute affair. Individuals on their own cannot usually command the necessary planning resources, allocate and organize the time required, or provide the desired degree of focus and direction.

It is not surprising, therefore, that educational institutions are becoming more interested in retirement planning programs for faculty and staff. The interest is relatively new. A 1978 survey of colleges and universities (Mulanaphy, p. vii) found that only 4 percent reported a formal program to help employees prepare for retirement. Although no subsequent survey has been made, there are indications of increased interest on the part of personnel officers and benefit plan administrators in the development and introduction of such programs (Olson, 1981, pp. 179–181).

The scope of existing retirement planning programs ranges from those providing a few sessions that explain retiring employees' benefits to formal, in-depth preparation programs that start some years prior to the institution's normal retirement age and continue over several months, with each session devoted to a particular topic and featuring invited experts. Mulanaphy (1978, pp. 61–63) notes the characteristics of an effective preretirement counseling program: (1) sufficient time for participants to make and implement plans, (2) voluntary participation, (3) open program eligibility, (4) content tailored to participants' needs, (5) flexibility (program adaptable to changes in employee composition, retirement rules, external developments), (6) attention to the human element, and (7) reinforcement and follow-up.

As to content, O'Meara (1977, pp. 37–38) has summarized program emphasis in terms of seven problem areas of retirement: health care, financial planning, housing arrangements, life-style adjustments, legal affairs, use of leisure time, and second careers.

With preparation for retirement increasingly recognized as a significant factor in retirement satisfaction, the value of the contributions of professionals in retirement planning has become evident. A number of organizations now provide a full array of services and materials for employer-sponsored programs for retirement planning. In addition, other organizations have prepared retirement planning workbooks and manuals for individuals or for use as supplements to organized employer-sponsored programs. An annotated list published by TIAA-CREF (1982a) summarizes retirement preparation programs and materials currently available.

## Summary

Recent developments in higher education have raised the possibility of how a college pension plan might facilitate increased rates of retirement prior to the stated normal age, and, among faculty who stay beyond the normal age, prior to the mandatory age. A review of a plan's current strength in providing benefits at the normal age — usually sixty-five — will enable determination of (1) the available base on which incentive early retirement programs can be built and (2) the current attractiveness of the plan for normal-age retirement.

Phased-retirement programs are another option, which, like early retirements, require coordination with regular pension provisions. Whether a retirement is early, phased, normal, or late, it should be arranged with attention to health insurance coverage in retirement and the benefits provided under the Social Security program. To be sufficiently attractive, incentive early-retirement programs and phased retirements must be flexible enough to meet a variety of individual financial and personal situations. Severance pay plans may be established as part of a plan offering supplemental early-retirement benefits.

Income from personal savings and investments accumulated prior to retirement can help make retirement more timely and more satisfying. A majority of educational institutions have set up tax-deferred annuity plans (TDAs) for extra savings in addition to their regular retirement plans. Under these plans, salary reduction agreements permit before-tax contributions to extra annuity benefits, with contributions and investment earnings free of federal income tax until received later. More recently, an additional tax-deferred retirement savings program has become available to employees. This is the Qualified Voluntary Employee Contribution Plan (QVEC), an alternative to the similar Individual Retirement Accounts (IRAs), but providing for contributions to an employer's regular or supplementary retirement plan through employee salary deduction.

Preretirement counseling programs and good employer communications regarding benefit programs can help contribute toward positive attitudes and plans for retirement. In the last few years, interest among educational employers in the development of formal retirement counseling programs has been growing rapidly.

## References

Association of American Colleges–American Association of University Professors (AAC-AAUP). "Statement of Principles on Academic Retirement and Insurance Plans." *Academe,* 1980, *66* (5), 321–323.

Bankers Trust Co. *Corporate Pension Plan Study: A Guide for the 1980s.* New York: Bankers Trust Co., 1980.

Bernstein, A. *1982 Tax Guide for College Teachers and Other College Personnel.* Washington, D.C.: Academic Information Service, 1981.

Consortium on Financing Higher Education. *The Report of the COFHE Study on Faculty Retirement: An Overview.* Cambridge, Mass.: Consortium on Financing Higher Education, 1980.

Cook, T. J. "College Benefit Plans and the Age Discrimination in Employment Act Amendments." *Academe,* 1981a, *67* (5), 308–312.

Cook, T. J. *Public Retirement Systems, Summaries of Public Retirement Plans Covering Colleges and Universities—1981.* New York: TIAA-CREF, 1981b.

Edwards, T. C. "NACUBO Report: Tom Edwards on TIAA-CREF." *Business Officer,* July 1982, pp. 11–13.

Employee Benefit Research Institute. *Tax Sheltered Annuities.* Washington, D.C.: Employee Benefit Research Institute, 1981.

*Federal Register,* May 25, 1979, *44,* p. 30648.

*Federal Register,* September 29, 1981, *46,* p. 47724.

Furniss, W. T. *Reshaping Faculty Careers.* Washington, D.C.: American Council on Education, 1981.

Heller, W. F. *Tax-Deferred Annuities for Employees of Exempt Organizations.* Philadelphia: American Law Institute–American Bar Association, 1979.

Jenny, H. H. *Early Retirement. A New Issue in Higher Education: The Financial Consequences of Early Retirement.* New York: TIAA-CREF, 1974.

Jenny, H. H., Heim, P., and Hughes, G. C. *Another Challenge, Age 70 Retirement in Higher Education.* New York: TIAA-CREF, 1979.

King, F. P., and Cook, T. J. *Benefit Plans in Higher Education.* New York: Columbia University Press, 1980.

McGill, D. M. *Fundamentals of Private Pensions.* Homewood, Ill.: Richard D. Irwin, 1975.

Mulanaphy, J. M. *1972–73 Survey of Retired TIAA-CREF Annuitants, Statistical Report.* New York: TIAA-CREF, 1974.

Mulanaphy, J. M. *Retirement Preparation in Higher Education.* New York: TIAA-CREF, 1978.

Mulanaphy, J. M. *Plans and Expectations for Retirement of TIAA-CREF Participants.* New York: TIAA-CREF, 1981.

National Center for Education Statistics. *Faculty Salaries, Tenure, and Benefits, 1980–81.* Washington, D.C.: National Center for Education Statistics, U. S. Department of Education, 1981.

Olson, S. K. "Current Status of Corporate Retirement Preparation Programs." *Aging and Work,* 1981, *4* (3), 175–187.

O'Meara, J. R. *Retirement: Reward or Rejection?* New York: Conference Board, 1977.

Social Security Administration, U.S. Department of Health and Human Services. *Social Security Handbook.* Washington, D.C.: U.S. Government Printing Office, 1982.

TIAA-CREF. "Social Security and TIAA-CREF Retirement Plans." *Bulletin,* December 1978.

TIAA-CREF. "Changes in Retirement Age Provisions." *The Participant,* March 1981, p. 2.

TIAA-CREF. *An Annotated List of Retirement Preparation Programs and Materials.* New York: TIAA-CREF, 1982a.

TIAA-CREF. *Supplemental Retirement Annuities for QVECs.* New York: TIAA-CREF, 1982b.

TIAA-CREF. *Tax-Deferred Annuities, Some Questions and Answers.* New York: TIAA-CREF, 1982c.

TIAA-CREF. *TIAA-CREF College and University Retirement Plan Provisions.* New York: TIAA-CREF, 1982d.

U.S. Congress, House Select Committee on Aging. "Effect of the Tenured Faculty Exemption in the 1978 ADEA Amendments." In *Abolishing Mandatory Retirement,*

*An Interim Report Prepared by the U.S. Department of Labor as Required by the Age Discrimination in Employment Act.* Comm. Pub. No. 97-283. Washington, D.C.: U.S. Government Printing Office, 1981.

*Note:* TIAA-CREF stands for Teachers Insurance and Annuity Association-College Retirement Equities Fund.

*Francis P. King is senior research officer of Teachers Insurance and Annuity Association–College Retirement Equities Fund.*

*Institutions need to take a fresh look at their faculty*
*personnel policies to insure that these are still responsive*
*to both individual and institutional needs and purposes.*

# Concluding Comments

*Jon W. Fuller*

## New Times Require New Policies

It would be surprising if the same faculty personnel policies that served the needs of institutions in times of expansion were to serve them as well in the more lean years that lie ahead. The point of this volume has been that these are good times to take another more comprehensive look at faculty personnel policies in each institution. Are those policies serving the basic purposes of the institution? Are they appropriate for the faculty members who now teach at each institution, and do they relate realistically to the experience of those faculty members?

These are times of apprehension and of an acute awareness of the limits of resources in many institutions. There is an obvious temptation for institutions, facing the prospect of enrollment decline and financial restrictions, to be more conservative and cautious, particularly in an area like faculty personnel policies. As the chapters of this volume have argued, however, this will in fact be a time that will demand greater flexibility and more creativity in the definition and administration of personnel policies.

It is important that a new awareness of limitations on resources not also serve to limit vision. Issues of faculty personnel policy may seem, at first, to be rather dry and technical. But they set the limits

J. W. Fuller (Ed.). *Issues in Faculty Personnel Policies.* New Directions for
Higher Education, no. 41. San Francisco: Jossey-Bass, March 1983.

within which faculty, who are at the heart of any higher education institution, carry on their work. It is important to attend to the influence that such policies have on the behavior of faculty, for that behavior will determine the vitality and effectiveness of an institution.

## Purposes of Good Personnel Policies

Good faculty personnel policies shape opportunities for individual growth and development. Inevitably, they will involve some risks by the institution. Conventional wisdom suggests that faculty personnel policies should be inherently conservative, designed to deal equitably with all individuals, to conserve institutional resources, and to meet the many requirements of law and regulation. But policies conceived with that narrow set of objectives will not effectively serve the larger purposes and objectives of most colleges and universities in the years ahead.

Good policies will require that a balance be struck by administrators and faculty committees who work on these issues, not only satisfying the demands for the prudent use of human resources and for meeting the requirements of law and equity, but also shaping an environment that encourages and helps faculty to remain lively and vigorous.

Where the appropriate kind of balance can be found, it may be possible, despite the gloomy external conditions which seem likely to face most institutions, to maintain educational programs that are vigorous and effective, led by faculty who are dedicated to their work and both enthusiastic and knowledgeable in their fields of scholarship and teaching.

## Tensions Between Individual and Institutional Needs

It is in the content of faculty personnel policies that the needs and objectives of the institution and the needs and objectives of individual faculty members are brought together. There is inevitably some tension between those individual and institutional needs, but well-designed institutional policies will finally succeed in serving both sets of needs well.

Tensions between individual and institutional perspectives appear from the beginning, even in the hiring process. Too often, colleges and universities see it as a *selection* procedure. But if an institution wants to attract the best candidates to its faculty, it needs to see that this requires *recruitment*, with the institution selling itself to the candidate it wants just as much as the candidates may be selling themselves to the institution. Female and minority candidates are particularly difficult for many institutions to attract, and sensitivity to their special concerns about an institution will enhance the chances of successfully recruiting them.

An institution needs to respond to the increasingly familiar problems of dual career couples, both in recruitment and in the terms of employment it offers. Various forms of joint or shared appointments are possible, as Louis Brakeman shows, and these are very useful in attracting some of the best candidates in today's academic marketplace.

Sensitivity to dual career issues also needs to extend to the administration of leave policies, as David Marker reminds us. The career requirements of a spouse and shared family responsibilities make it difficult for more and more faculty to leave home during leaves, even when the best opportunities for personal and professional development are elsewhere.

The case for flexibility in the use of leaves, particularly to allow faculty members to explore new directions for their careers, is discussed by both David Marker and Roger Baldwin in their respective chapters. But administrators and faculty committees will see these suggestions as a clear case of conflict between individual and institutional needs and purposes. Faculty members have traditionally been granted leaves in order that they may return to the campus with new knowledge and enthusiasm to apply to their teaching and scholarship. It is true that many sabbaticals have been used covertly to explore new career possibilities, and that few institutions have wanted to require a faculty member to return unwillingly for the agreed period of service back on campus. But explicit approval of leaves for such purposes is difficult for many to accept. It will be possible only if seen in light of institutional interests in the continued renewal of faculty members throughout their careers and in the encouragement of some greater turnover in faculty ranks during these times of retrenchment in order to make some room for appointments of faculty with needed new skills and training.

Even many of the issues in faculty evaluation turn on differences between institutional and individual purposes. When individuals overcome their initial temptation simply to ask to be left alone, they will be most attracted to evaluation plans that support individual professional growth and development. The institution, on the other hand, needs the results of evaluation to provide a defensible and objective basis for salary, promotion, and tenure decisions. As Kala Stroup notes in her discussion of these issues, no single scheme of evaluation is likely to serve these differing purposes — an argument for using some combination of methods.

Compensation issues present their own complexity. Salary policies are pulled one way by demands within the institution for equity and a different way by an external labor market in which faculty from some disciplines command substantially different salaries than those in other disciplines. The increasing variety of fringe benefits adds to the complexity of compensation policy, so that the variety of technical issues which are raised may obscure the larger institutional purposes which should be served. Fred Silander reminds us that compensation policy can and should serve institutional purposes, particularly in attracting and retaining the best possible faculty.

Roger Baldwin argues for flexibility in a number of personnel policies and practices in order to provide the variety that most faculty members need over the course of their careers. While this might be seen primarily as serving individual interests, it takes on an institutional purpose as well when it is recognized that most faculty members, once tenured, will spend their entire careers at a single institution. Colleges and universities have a stake in the continued vitality and effectiveness of all their faculty.

Even providing attractive options in the retirement plan and insuring adequate pension levels serves institutional as well as individual purposes, as Francis King explains. Individuals need to be encouraged to plan for each new stage of their careers, including that final stage represented by retirement. If appropriate options are offered, and sufficient funding provided, individuals will be more likely to make retirement decisions in their own best interests and in the best interests of their institutions as well.

## Problems of Complexity

Many issues of faculty personnel policy are painfully complex. Administrators and faculty members often find it difficult to know just what an institution can and cannot do in setting policies to serve institutional needs while also meeting the requirements of law and regulation. Continued gaps in our knowledge about the process of teaching and learning leave us without fully satisfactory methods to evaluate faculty performance either to encourage continued professional growth and improvement or to provide a fair basis for recognition and reward. A similar complexity may restrain institutions seeking to provide new options and incentives in their retirement programs. And as forms of fringe benefits multiply, issues of compensation become more difficult to understand and administer.

It is important that this inevitable complexity not cause us to deal with personnel policies primarily in terms of narrow technical issues. They must be addressed in terms of the broader institutional objectives which should be served.

## Shaping Appropriate Faculty Personnel Policies

The chapters of this volume illustrate the difficulties of arriving at sound personnel policies for faculty in today's colleges and universities. It is hoped that these chapters also provide useful and specific suggestions about how those policies can be reshaped to keep them responsive to both institutional and individual needs and purposes.

The principal theme of the volume has been that such policies should not be viewed primarily as technical issues. Nor should they be approached in a spirit of caution and apprehension. Rather, they can be seen as an opportunity to set out the framework for recruiting good faculty and sustaining them through useful, satisfying, and productive careers.

*Jon W. Fuller is president of the Great Lakes Colleges Association (GLCA), a consortium of twelve liberal arts colleges in Indiana, Michigan, and Ohio.*

# Index